Killer Smog

By William Wise

Killer Smog

THE WORLD'S WORST AIR POLLUTION DISASTER

AN AUTHORS GUILD BACKINPRINT.COM EDITION

Killer Smog

The World's Worst Air Pollution Disaster

AN AUTHORS GUILD BACKINPRINT.COM EDITION

Published by iUniverse.com, Inc.

For information address:
iUniverse.com, Inc.
5220 S 16th, Ste. 200
Lincoln, NE 68512
www.iuniverse.com

Originally published by Rand McNally

ISBN: 0-595-17184-2

Printed in the United States of America

"The London 'smog' was accompanied by an immediate and sudden rise in both illness and mortality. The number of deaths over and above those normally expected in the first three weeks of December indicates that some 4,000 people died as a result of the 'smog.'"

Committee on Air Pollution,
INTERIM REPORT, December, 1953.

"We are just as close to an air pollution disaster as we were last Thanksgiving."

Senator Robert F. Kennedy,
THE NEW YORK TIMES, 20 June, 1967.

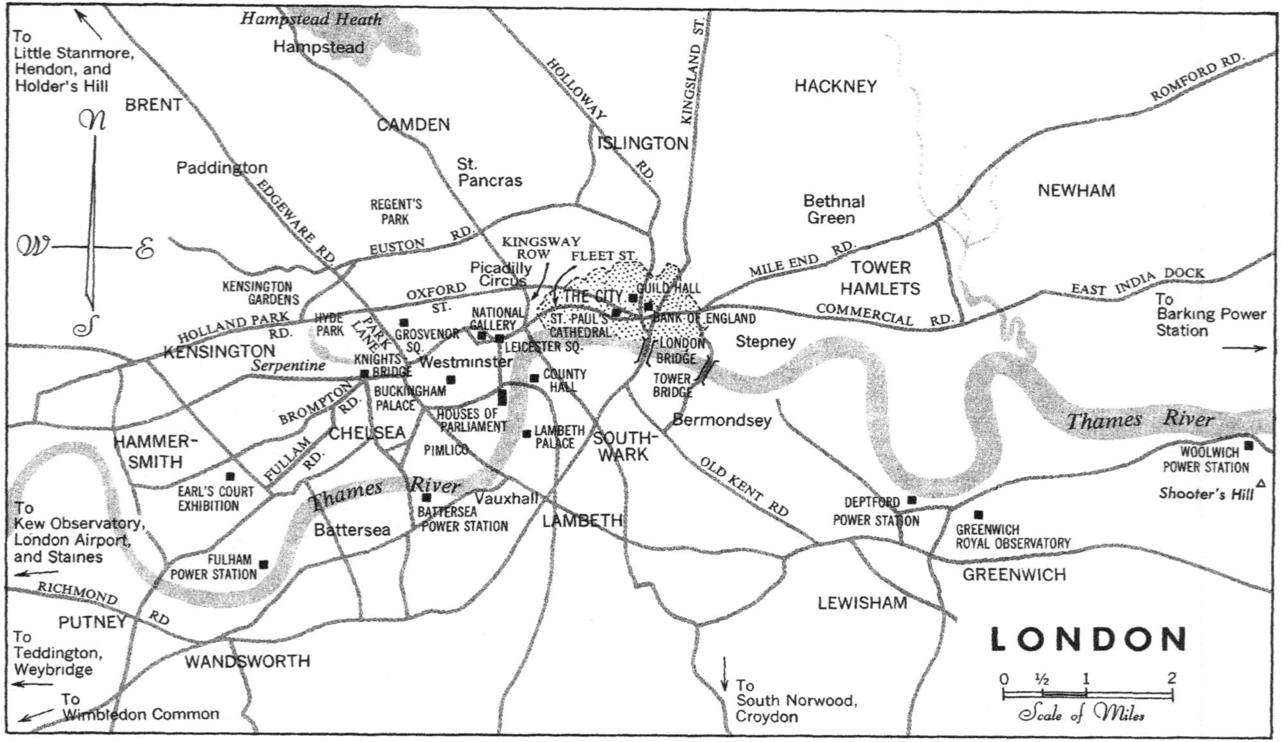

LONDON
To Little Stanmore, Hendon, and Holder's Hill
Hampstead Heath
Hampstead
BRENT
CAMDEN
HOLLOWAY RD.
KINGSLAND ST.
HACKNEY
ISLINGTON
ROMFORD RD.
Paddington
St. Pancras
EDGEWARE RD
REGENT'S PARK
Bethnal Green
NEWHAM
EUSTON RD.
KINGSWAY ROW
FLEET ST.
MILE END RD.
TOWER HAMLETS
Picadilly Circus
KENSINGTON GARDENS
OXFORD ST.
THE CITY
GUILD HALL
EAST INDIA DOCK
To Barking Power Station
ST. PAUL'S CATHEDRAL
BANK OF ENGLAND
COMMERCIAL RD.
HOLLAND PARK RD.
HYDE PARK
PARK LANE
GROSVENOR SQ.
NATIONAL GALLERY
LEICESTER SQ.
LONDON BRIDGE
Stepney
KENSINGTON
Serpentine
KNIGHTSBRIDGE
Westminster
COUNTY HALL
TOWER BRIDGE
BUCKINGHAM PALACE
BROMPTON RD.
HOUSES OF PARLIAMENT
Bermondsey
Thames River
CHELSEA
LAMBETH PALACE
SOUTHWARK
HAMMERSMITH
PIMLICO
OLD KENT RD
WOOLWICH POWER STATION
FULLAM RD.
EARL'S COURT EXHIBITION
Shooter's Hill
Vauxhall
DEPTFORD POWER STATION
To Kew Observatory, London Airport, and Staines
BATTERSEA POWER STATION
LAMBETH
Battersea
GREENWICH ROYAL OBSERVATORY
FULHAM POWER STATION
GREENWICH
RICHMOND RD
LEWISHAM
PUTNEY
To Teddington, Weybridge
WANDSWORTH
To South Norwood, Croydon
To Wimbledon Common
0 ½ 1 2
Scale of Miles
N
W
E
S

Acknowledgments

WHILE GATHERING material for *Killer Smog* I received information, advice, and assistance from many organizations and individuals—I am grateful to all of them. Among the organizations, the British Information Service in New York City, and London's National Society for Clean Air—formerly the National Smoke Abatement Society—were especially helpful. My thanks also to the New York Society Library, the New York Academy of Medicine, and the New York Public Library, and to the London Emergency Bed Service, the London Weather Centre, the Thames Navigation Service, the Metropolitan Police, the Central Electricity Generating Board, the Automobile Association, the Greater London Council, the British Broadcasting Corporation, the London Ambulance Service, and to numerous London Borough Councils and their officers, for the kindness and cooperation they extended to me during my stay in London.

For their courtesy and help, I would also like to thank the late Sir Hugh Beaver, Sir Gerald Nabarro, Mr. Arnold Marsh, Mr. K. S. Morfey, Miss Ruth Isaacs, and Drs. William Stott, Mary Adams, Caroline Meade, M. M. Scott, John Fry, Audrey Hanson, and Michael Rosenbluth—in a variety of ways, the aid of each was most useful.

Among dozens of others who generously provided assistance were: Dr. George Abercrombie, Dr. Fred Becker, Mrs. Pauline Clouston, Mr. W. E. Cooke, Mr. John Creasy, Dr. Cecil Coyle, Dr. Reginald DeWar, Dr. W. R. Doll, Mr. P. B. Ediss, Dr. J. E. Epsom, Mrs. V. Finlay, Dr. Victor Freeman, Miss Margaret Gale, Captain W. Gregson, Mr. Mark Hamilton, Mr. C. C. Hitchen, Dr. Patrick J. Lawther, Mr. Clifford Longden, Commander G. V. Parmiter, Mr. R. E. Peers, Miss Margaret Radcliffe, Mr. Percy Scarisbrick, Mr. F. W. Skelcher, and Mr. A. M. Smith.

Finally, I would like to express my gratitude to Mrs. Cynthia Smith Vartan, for her unfailing patience, understanding, and encouragement during the writing of this book. No editor could have been more steadfast—no writer more fortunate.

William Wise

Note: All the people described in Part Two, Anatomy of a Disaster, have been given fictional names, and their places of residence or work have been similarly altered. For the sake of clarity and conciseness, a limited amount of material has been elided, and one person's fragmentary recollection becomes part of somebody else's broader and more meaningful experience.

Killer Smog

Part One:

Cause for Alarm

". . . the London fog of December, 1952, was no strange new phenomenon. It was no acute epidemic caused by a hitherto unrecognized virus nor was it a visitation of some known pathogen against which we had no defence. It was simply the occurrence of a well known meteorological phenomenon in an area where the toxic products of combustion are vomited in excess into the air. . . ."

THE MEDICAL OFFICER,
14 February, 1953.

Chapter One

ONE BLUSTERY MORNING in late November, 1966, I found myself at London Airport, boarding a plane for the United States and home. I'd been in England a number of weeks, a writer gathering information about the notorious London smog of December, 1952. Most of the people I'd interviewed had been patient and helpful. A few had also been openly skeptical.

Why, the doubters had wanted to know, was I investigating London's "Killer Smog" of a decade-and-a-half before? Would the story of that landmark disaster be likely to prove very meaningful to an American audience? Was smog of much concern to my fellow countrymen? They were only asking me because—well, surely in the States, with the exception of Los Angeles, of course—we Americans didn't really *have* any smog, did we?

The doubters should have been aboard my plane later in the day. Approaching Kennedy Airport, in New York, we were told there would be a half-hour's delay in landing. Puzzled, I raised the plastic window shade and peered out.

We were flying at about two thousand feet, through a curiously greasy-looking and pervasive haze. The ground could just be made out below—cars, roads, houses, all dim but visible.

Then we began to climb. In less than a minute the ground had vanished. Cars, roads, houses, the very earth itself had been blotted out. We were circling in bright sunlight, above an apparently limitless bank of opaque, polluted air. The smog extended to the horizon in every direction. At a distance, the slanting rays of the sun gave it a coppery, rather handsome appearance. Nearer at hand it merely looked yellow and ugly, like nothing so much as a vast and unappetizing sea of chicken soup.

Such was the air which the people of New York, Connecticut, and New Jersey were compelled to breathe for three consecutive days and nights during Thanksgiving weekend, 1966. Newly born infants, the old, the infirm—all were subjected to a poisoned atmosphere which at one measuring station contained five times the "normal" level of sulfur dioxide. At the same station smoke and deadly carbon monoxide were recorded in amounts above the "danger" level.

Nor was this the first acute air pollution episode the area's inhabitants had experienced. In 1953, an estimated 240 people had been killed in New York City alone by a ismilar mass of stagnant, filthy air; a decade later more than 400 excess deaths were reported in the city during a five-day smog. In neither instance was there any way of calculating how many additional victims had been killed in other communities along America's East Coast or how many thousands, from Washington, D.C., in the south, to Massachusetts in the north, had been made severely ill.

Was smog of much concern to my fellow countrymen. . . ?

Eight months prior to New York's Thanksgiving Smog of 1966, Dr. Walter Orr Roberts, director of America's National Center for Atmospheric Research, had spoken of the imminent likelihood of an air pollution disaster taking place somewhere in the world which would kill as many as ten thousand people. Almost any large industrial center, the doctor had said, might well provide the setting for such a deadly smog. Particularly vulnerable foreign cities included London; Hamburg, Germany; and Santiago, Chile; in the United States, Los Angeles and New York were the most obvious candidates.

Shortly before the Thanksgiving smog, Dr. Roberts was asked whether he believed that *many* of America's cities were vulnerable to a disaster similar to London's great killer smog of 1952. "Yes," he replied, "I have been worried . . . that we might wake up some morning in some major city to an unusual meteorological situation . . . that prevented the air from circulating . . . and that we might find thousands of people dead as the result of the air they were forced to breathe in that smog situation."

Why, the doubters had wanted to know, was I investigating London's killer smog of a decade-and-a-half before? Surely in the States, we Americans didn't really have any smog, did we...?

Anyone aboard a plane arriving in New York on the twenty-third of November would have been able to answer for himself.

Two

THE METEOROLOGICAL CONDITIONS immediately responsible for London's great killer smog began to develop on Thursday, the fourth of December, 1952. It was then that an extensive high-pressure weather system spread slowly, in a southeasterly direction, across most of the British Isles. The system brought with it light variable winds, dry air, and rather frigid temperatures. At dusk its center lay a little more than two hundred miles to the northwest of the capital and the gently sloping valley of the Thames.

After sundown, the light breezes began to fail. By midnight, instruments on the roof of the Air Ministry building at Kingsway, in the heart of London, could record a wind velocity of only two knots an hour. At Kew Observatory, in the western part of the city, there was no wind velocity at all.

During the night many sections of the almost windless valley experienced a temperature inversion; air near the ground grew colder; soon, it was trapped beneath a lid of warmer air above. Unable to rise vertically, and with no wind to disperse it laterally, the shallow layer of low-lying, frigid air was now totally inert. London found itself becalmed. It was destined to remain so, almost without remission, for a period of four days and nights.

Considerable fog began to form late Thursday evening and during the early hours of Friday morning. At first it remained comparatively clean and harmless—but not for long. As the city awoke, tons of smoke from millions of domestic chimneys were hurled upward into the cold, motionless, foggy air. Huge power stations added still more tons of coal smoke and sulfur oxides to the atmosphere. Cars, trucks, buses, and a variety of factories and industrial plants all contributed their pollutants. In a short time the fog had become massively contaminated by a mixture of smoke, soot, carbon particles, and gaseous wastes. Now yellow, now amber, now black, the great killer smog held London in its grip, and by early evening, only twelve hours after its onset, the first of the city's inhabitants began to die.

The full toll of human life exacted by London's worst air pollution disaster was never determined. Results of a belated statistical investigation, conducted for the government by the Ministry of Health, indicated that nearly one out of every two thousand people in the city either perished during the four-day smog or else succumbed during the following two weeks.

These, however, were not the only victims. In addition, thousands of Londoners became seriously ill, recovered temporarily, and then died, months or even years later. To what extent their lives had been shortened by the destructive effects of the smog, no governmental or private organization could afterward say, and indeed, no particular effort was ever made to examine the matter.

An official study of the killer smog, published more than a year after the event, disclosed considerable information about the nature and dimensions of the tragedy; it also left a number of important questions unanswered. Curiously, the most searching question of all was never even raised: why, in the light of prior knowledge and despite both old and recent warnings, had no one in a position of influence or authority made a serious attempt to forestall the disaster? Because one thing was certain: London's foggy climate, her many industrial plants, her inefficient, coal-burning domestic chimneys, and her long history of smoky, polluted air, all made the formation of a vast killer smog extremely likely; the omens were clear, had anyone cared to read them.

Yet, when the great killer smog finally came, it caught London and the nation by surprise. Perhaps that was the most incomprehensible thing about it.

Three

THE ATMOSPHERE of Great Britain's commercial cities, and particularly of London, has been polluted by man for many centuries. More than seven hundred years ago, when the present metropolis was still only a walled, medieval town, visitors often became aware, thanks to a sudden shift in the wind, of the unusually acrid and smoky fumes assaulting their nostrils. Long before such notable events as the discovery of America or the invention of printing, the air of London Town had already gained a widespread and distinctly unfavorable reputation.

London's air pollution problems began during Plantagenet times, with the introduction of bituminous coal into the city. The step was an economic one. By late in the twelfth century the great forests were growing smaller and the price of wood, at least in the vicinity of London, had increased considerably. An additional source of fuel was needed for manufacturing; the fuel had to be cheap and easily obtainable. "Sea coal"—as it then was called because several large outcroppings had been found by the northeast seacoast and the Firth of Forth—proved to be a convenient substitute. Soon, London's brewers, smiths, dyers, and other artisans were burning the new sea coal in their kilns and furnaces. By 1228 the practice was fairly general, for in that year there was a suburban byway outside the town which bore the name of Sacoles—or Sea Coals—Lane.

Although the brewers and smiths were pleased by the cheapness of the new fuel and by the ease with which it could be burned, the rest of the populace did not show a corresponding enthusiasm. "By the bulk of the community," Robert L. Galloway says in his *A History of Coal Mining, in Great Britain;* "coal fuel was regarded with much aversion on account of the disagreeable smoke to which it gave rise. Coal smoke was considered to be very detrimental to health. It began to be considered a source of annoyance while the coal trade was still in its infancy."

It wasn't long before complaints were being made, although the earliest one on record was not directed against the city of London. In 1257, Queen Eleanor was staying in Nottingham, while her husband, Henry III, was absent in Wales at the head of his army. The smoke of the city was too much for the queen. She protested that Nottingham was uninhabitable, and shortly afterward departed for the cleaner air of Tutbury Castle, twenty-five miles away.

By the end of the thirteenth century, agitation against London's smoky atmosphere had become quite vigorous. It was led by various important noblemen and clerics who came to neighboring Westminster to attend Parliament. The public supported their protests, with the result that in 1306 the royal favor was won; and a proclamation was issued in the name of Edward I, drastically curtailing the use of coal in the city. It was the British government's first attempt at controlling air pollution.

Edward Longshanks' proclamation was clear in its purpose and severe in its penalties. It prohibited London's artisans and manufacturers from using coal in their furnaces during sessions of Parliament and ordered them, instead, to return to their former practice of burning wood. One miscreant, caught with warm coals in his furnace, was duly executed.

The harshness of his sentence had no effect on his fellow artisans. They persisted in using coal out of season as well as in, so that by the next year a commission was appointed "to inquire of all who burnt sea coal in the city, or parts adjoining, and to punish them for the first offense with great fines and ransoms, and upon the second offense to demolish their furnaces." This measure was a failure, too. Bituminous coal remained abundant and cheap, and so it continued to be employed in manufacturing.

As a domestic fuel, however, coal did not come into common use for another century or two. It was staunchly resisted at first because of its sulfurous odor and the irritation it caused the throat and lungs of anyone who inhaled its smoke. But as the price of wood continued to rise, resistance crumbled. For the sake of economy the poorer classes began to burn coal in their homes during the fifteenth and sixteenth centuries.

Meanwhile, London's air grew darker and more unhealthy. In 1578 the city's Company of Brewers agreed to burn nothing but wood in their brewhouses—situated, unhappily, quite near Westminster Palace—because Elizabeth the queen "findeth herself greatly grieved and annoyed by the taste and smoke of the sea coals."

Still later in Elizabeth's reign, a royal proclamation was published, once more forbidding the use of coal in London while Parliament was sitting. In 1595, an entrepreneur named Thomas Owen offered to transport clean-burning anthracite from distant Wales to help rid the city of smoke.

But anthracite would have been more expensive than bituminous coal, and nothing more was heard of Owen's proposal.

By the reign of James I, wood was becoming too dear a fuel for even the wealthiest London families to burn in their homes. Writing about the changes which had occurred during his own lifetime, an early social commentator named Howes reported fierce opposition to the use of coal as late as 1600; in that year, "the nice dames of London would not come into any house or room where sea coals were burned, nor willingly eat of the meat that was roast with the coal fire." Such opposition, Howes added, soon disappeared. In another decade, polite society decided to accept the inevitable, and holding its collective fingers to its offended nose, began to buy coal for cooking and heating purposes.

There was no improvement in the city's air by the middle of the century. The year 1648 saw a group of afflicted Londoners petitioning Parliament for a law prohibiting the importation of coal from Newcastle. Like most such petitions, it produced no results whatever.

And then, in 1661, an idealistic London citizen, the noted diarist John Evelyn, decided to circulate a pamphlet. Published the same year, it was a short volume with a very long title: *Fumifugium, or, the Inconvenience of the Air, and Smoke of London Dissipated. Together with some Remedies humbly proposed by J.E. Esq., to his Sacred Majesty, and to the Parliament now Assembled.*

The *Smoke of London* became a minor classic to later generations. Though often out of print, it was never entirely forgotten. Today, with its elaborate phrases and its old-fashioned language, it seems, at first glance, to be merely an antiquarian's curiosity. Yet, disquietingly enough, the work deals with matters that are contemporary and familiar —suggesting that the lords and governors of the modern world still have not learned how to effectively solve, in the 1960's, some of the identical problems that vexed the rulers of Britain, a full three hundred years ago.

Four

JOHN EVELYN was proud of London's preeminence, the splendor of her public buildings, and the still-rural charms of her orchards, gardens, and fields. But this did not blind him to the city's dirt and grime, her increasing squalor, and the high incidence of disease among her inhabitants.

A confirmed Royalist, Evelyn was often present at the palace in Whitehall. One afternoon he happened to overhear Charles II inveighing against the thick, smoky air so prevalent in London. Encouraged by the king's remarks, Evelyn returned home and soon had composed an informal survey of conditions in the city, adding to it a scheme for making the palace and its surroundings a more enjoyable place to live.

The *Smoke of London* began with a courtier's flattery. "Sir, it was one day," Evelyn wrote, "as I was walking in Your Majesty's Palace at Whitehall (where I have sometimes the honor to refresh myself with the sight of Your Illustrious Presence, which is the joy of Your People's hearts) that a presumptuous smoke issuing from near Northumberland-house, and not far from Scotland-yard, did so invade the Court, that all the rooms, galleries and places about it, were filled and infested with it, and that to such a degree as men could hardly discern one another from the cloud, and none could support, without manifest inconvenience. It was this alone and the trouble that it needs must [give] to Your Sacred Majesty, as well as the hazard to Your Health, which kindled this indignation of mine. Nor must I forget that Illustrious and Divine Princess, Your Majesty's only Sister, the now Duchess of Orleans, who, late being in this city, did in my hearing, complain of the effects of this smoke both in her breast and lungs, whilst she was in Your Majesty's Palace."

But the polluted air was not confined to Whitehall, and Evelyn, having paid sufficient homage to the royal family, could then set about the task of describing the ills of the entire community. "That this glorious and ancient city," he wrote, "which commands the proud ocean to the Indies, and reaches the farthest Antipodes, should wrap her stately head in clouds of smoke and sulphur, so full of stink and darkness, I deplore."

Bituminous coal was employed without restriction, Evelyn believed, because of men's greed. The chief culprits were the merchants who imported it and the manufacturers who used it in their furnaces, principally the city's brewers, dyers, lime-burners, and soap- and salt-boilers.

Of all the cities in the world, Evelyn said, London should have been the most glorious in which to live. Her location, on a hill overlooking the broad and beautiful Thames, her wide suburban avenues, her stately buildings and noble palaces, all contributed to her natural grandeur. Yet life in London held little that was glorious or grand; most often it was a disagreeable, unhealthy affair. Evelyn blamed the pervasive smoke, which he called "this hellish and dismal cloud of sea coal," and which he said, "is so universally mixed with the otherwise wholesome and excellent air that [Londoners] breathe nothing but an impure and thick mist, accompanied by a fuliginous and filthy vapor, corrupting the lungs, so that catarrhs, coughs and consumptions rage more in this one city, than in the whole Earth."

The coal smoke, Evelyn continued, made London resemble "the face of Mount Etna, the Court of Vulcan, Stromboli, or the Suburbs of Hell, rather than an assembly of rational creatures, and the imperial seat of our incomparable Monarch. For when in all other places the air is most serene and pure, it is here eclipsed with such a cloud of sulphur, as the sun itself, which gives day to all the world, is hardly able to penetrate, and the weary traveller, at many miles distance, sooner smells, than sees the city to which he repairs.

"This is that pernicious smoke which sullies all of

[London's] glory, superinducing a sooty crust or fur upon all that it [touches], spoiling the movables, tarnishing the plate, gildings and furniture, and corroding the iron-bars and hardest stones."

Medical experts in the twentieth century tend to be cautious; some authorities reluctantly concede that chronic air pollution may be harmful to even healthy human lungs but insist that until the question has been determined to their complete statistical satisfaction, through controlled scientific tests, and to the last one thousandth of a percentage point, they would prefer not to take too firm a stand or to complain too passionately about the dirty air which their fellow citizens are daily forced to breathe. Evelyn, not burdened by their modern scientific outlook, was content to use a more ready rule of thumb. London's air was undeniably foul—he himself had choked on it often enough—and since the people of London plainly suffered a disproportionate amount of respiratory disease, the connection, though perhaps incapable of exact measurement, seemed perfectly clear to his innocent, seventeenth-century mind.

The result of Londoners being compelled to breathe smoke and sulfurous gases, Evelyn said, "is that almost half of them who perish in London die of [consumptive] and [pulmonary] distempers, that the inhabitants are never free from coughs and importunate rheumatisms, and the spitting of impostumate and corrupt matter. Is there under Heaven such coughing and snuffing to be heard, as in the London churches and assemblies of people, where the barking and spitting is incessant?"

Evelyn knew that the poisoned atmosphere of London could kill slowly or swiftly. There was a famous old man named Parr, he reminded his readers, a legendary fellow who had lived in good health for more than a century—in the country. Then Parr had decided to visit London. Some people maintained that the change of diet had killed him, but Evelyn insisted it was the foul air "which plainly withered him, and spoiled his digestion in a short time after his arrival."

The atmosphere of the city was becoming so bad that to avoid breathing it, some of the wealthier families were resorting to a twentieth-century expedient—they were moving to the suburbs. Evelyn learned of one individual "who had so strange an antipathy to the air of London, that though he were a merchant, and had frequent business in the city, was yet constrained to make his dwelling some miles outside; and when he came to the Exchange, within an hour or two, he grew so extremely indisposed, that he was forced to take horse and ride for his life, till he came into the fields."

The effect on human health, Evelyn said, could be inferred, by examining the damage to plant life within the city. In 1644, during the civil war, Newcastle had been besieged, and hardly any coal had reached London. That year, "divers gardens and orchards, planted in the very heart of London, were observed to bear such plentiful and infinite quantities of fruits, as they were never produced either before or since. It was rightly imputed by the owners to the little smoke—argument sufficient to demonstrate how prejudicial it is to the bodies of men."

The solution to London's polluted air, Evelyn explained, was to shut down the furnaces and kilns, the breweries, the lime-burning establishments, the other offenders, and move them all at least six miles outside the city—and away from the prevailing winds. Since coal would still be burned in private homes, and since some pollution would still exist, a great number of flowering trees and aromatic shrubs were to be planted around the city's perimeter and within the city itself. The result would be to perfume London, as Paris was perfumed during the rose season or Genoa, during orange-blossom time.

Evelyn felt optimistic about the chances for reform when he offered his suggestions to the king and Parliament. "I see the dawning of a brighter day approach," he wrote. "We have a Prince who is resolved to be a *Father to his Country*, and a Parliament whose decrees take their impression from his Majesty's great genius, which studies only the Public Good. It is from them, therefore, that we augur our future happiness; since there is nothing which will so perpetuate their memories, or more justly merit it."

The breweries and lime kilns were not moved six miles out of the city. No flowering trees or aromatic shrubs were planted. The air remained as poisonous as it had been before, and the inhabitants of London continued to cough, spit, and die. For all the effect it had produced, the *Smoke of London* might never have been written.

Five

JOHN EVELYN apparently was blessed with robust health and an excellent pair of lungs. He lived on to the age of eighty-six, recording conscientiously in his diaries, year after year, the changing patterns of London life and the most striking public events as they occurred.

Evelyn was present in 1665, when the Great Plague killed 20 percent of the population within the walls and many additional thousands in the surrounding villages. He was in London the following September, as the Great Fire, from its modest beginnings in a baker's shop in Pudding Lane, grew into the vast conflagration which ultimately destroyed three-quarters of the old medieval town. Included in the destruction, besides the Royal Exchange and Guildhall, were thirteen thousand dwelling houses, eighty-nine churches, and the city's cathedral. Six months later, the diarist observed that the cellars and other ruins of the town were still smoldering. The streets themselves remained so hot he scorched the soles of his shoes as he walked about on a tour of inspection.

Both Sir Christopher Wren and John Evelyn submitted comprehensive plans for rebuilding the city, but their ideas were not closely adhered to. London already was a great port and commercial center, and the needs of business could not wait, idle and unattended, while city planners decided what should be done. Nor was there money available to buy extra land, so that the prospective streets and buildings could be laid out according to Wren's or Evelyn's spacious designs. Instead, the city began to grow up again, helter-skelter, without an overall scheme.

The full process of restoration, though, was to prove a long one. For thirty or forty years the center of London remained an ever-shrinking collection of ruins, overgrown with wild flowers and weeds, while here and there in the midst of the desolation another new building would begin to rise.

But in time it did become plain that the rebuilt city was to be a considerably more agreeable place in which to live than the old walled town. Its dwellings were less cramped, they were constructed of stronger materials, and sometimes they possessed a bit of open land around them. The streets were somewhat wider and received more sunlight, and because the overcrowding had been reduced, the inhabitants were less subject to epidemic disease. But the problem of dirty air was in no way improved. Greater and greater quantities of coal continued to be consumed, and the increasing volume of smoke and sulfur dioxide remained a blight on the daily lives of the inhabitants.

January, 1684, was exceptionally cold in London. There was a period of subfreezing weather, lasting several weeks. The Thames became frozen, most solidly above venerable London Bridge, whose narrow piers and arches slowed the current of the river and helped to form a broad, still lake upstream.

On January 9, Evelyn noted the exceptionally bitter weather. "I went across the Thames on the ice," he wrote, "now become so thick as to bear not only streets of booths in which they roast meat, and had divers shops of wares, but coaches, carts and horses pass over. So I went from Westminster Stairs to Lambeth, and dined with the Archbishop."

Two weeks later, Evelyn observed something else. Unaware of its implications for the future, he described, perhaps for the first time anywhere, a thermal, or temperature, inversion—that meteorological phenomenon which invariably accompanies smog disasters—and the effect that it had on the respiration of even so hale a person as himself.

"London," Evelyn said, "by reason of the excessive coldness of the air hindering the ascent of the smoke, was so filled with the fuliginous steam of the sea coal, that one could hardly see across the streets, and this filling the lungs with its gross particles, exceedingly obstructed the breast, so as one could hardly breathe."

Clearly, in the time of the Stuarts, air pollution, in conjunction with severe winter weather, already menaced any Londoner unfortunate enough to suffer from a chronic chest complaint such as asthma, bronchitis, or emphysema. Today, one hears it said that poisoned air has only recently become a public health problem, otherwise it surely would have been studied and curbed a long time ago. Perhaps the assertion would be more persuasive if it also happened to be true.

Six

IN THE DECADES immediately following the Great Fire, a number of new areas in the vicinity of London were opened to development. To the west of the old city many acres of formerly empty fields and marshes were settled, the fashionable world taking up residence in St. James's, Bloomsbury, and Soho Squares, while at the same time wealthy city merchants built comfortable country houses, with spacious gardens, in a number of villages on London's outskirts. The suburban villages themselves, as well as the city of Westminster and the Borough of Southwark, expanded in both size and population; as they did, and as the old city spread to the east, the outlines of the future metropolis first began to emerge.

During the same period, London continued to grow in

importance as a financial center. The city had long been a major port; now, it was rapidly becoming Amsterdam's chief rival for the leadership of European commerce. The great Chartered Companies flourished in the city, and shipping of every description crowded the Thames.

The coal trade was enlarging with all the rest; according to Daniel Defoe's calculations, the port of London received almost thirty million bushels of coal each year from Newcastle and the coasts of Durham and Northumberland. Ships employed to transport coal were called cats, hags, or hagboats. During wartime, or when there had been unfavorable winds to delay their passage, as many as six or seven hundred of these boats might arrive in London on the same day. From the docks, the coals were carried to the coal exchange, where they were measured under the supervision of the Lord Mayor. Then they were passed on to the coal brokers, known by the unappealing name of "crimps," who had no difficulty in finding customers, because in London, as Defoe said, the coals "never want a market."

London and the Thames valley had always been subject to brief spells of clean, natural fog. But the growth of the city and the attendant rise in the use of coal began to change this benign phenomenon into something more sinister; for coal, inefficiently burned, produces large volumes of smoke, which will not only mingle with fog and pollute it but will also thicken it and greatly prolong its life. By the close of the seventeenth century, the fogs of London already were remarkable for their density and duration. They were, indeed, a rather primitive and uncomplicated variant of what is called in our own time "a modern urban-industrial smog."

In 1699, almost at the end of his life, John Evelyn noted that the fogs in the city had become so thick they offered a number of hazards to the traveler which had been unknown in his own youth. Because of their dark obscurity an honest citizen was likely to lose his way in the streets and fall into the hands of footpads or thieves. If, instead, he chose to leave the streets and take to the fogbound river, he might find himself in even greater peril; for then, although drums were beaten on the shore to guide his boatman to safety, a collision could not always be avoided and sometimes both traveler and boatman went over the side to drown in the icy waters of the Thames.

Winter or summer, fall or spring, the unwholesomeness of the city's atmosphere continued to grow. For a time, some of the outlying villages, like Kensington, Hampstead, and Paddington, remained primarily rural and served as temporary refuges for Londoners in search of cleaner air. In 1722, a minor poet, Thomas Tickell, could still describe the daily springtime excursions of fashionable ladies to Kensington Gardens in the vicinity of the palace:

Where Kensington, high o'er the neighbouring lands
Midst greens and sweets, a regal fabric, stands,
And sees each spring, luxuriant in her bowers,
A snow of blossoms, and a wild of flowers,
The dames of Britain oft in crowds repair
To gravel walks, and unpolluted air.
Here, while the town in damps and darkness lies,
They breathe in sunshine, and see azure skies.

But days of sunshine and azure skies were destined to become rarer, even in rural Kensington. Forty years after Evelyn's death, the city had experienced a further expansion. Berkeley and Grosvenor Squares had been completed in the West End, and handsome new houses were beginning to appear along Park Lane. The suburbs of Bethnal Green, Hackney, and Islington were more thickly settled, and there was less open country between Paddington and Hampstead and the center of London.

The air, quite naturally, had grown smokier, and the fogs had become thicker, for there were now more and more people living in London, and each year they burned more and more raw coal. The city's manufacturing plants had multiplied as well, to be joined by new industries which had not even existed in Evelyn's day.

In 1772, more than a hundred years after the *Smoke of London* had originally appeared, a new edition was prepared for the press. The editor, Mr. White, included a preface of his own; it indicated that the problem of the city's poisoned air had become even graver during the intervening century.

"The established reputation of Mr. Evelyn's writings," the new edition began, "would have prevented the Editor from adding anything himself, had not time made some alterations that appear worthy of notice.

"[In the original edition, Mr. Evelyn] expresses himself with proper warmth and indignation against the absurd policy of allowing brewers, dyers, soap-boilers and lime-burners to intermix their noisesome works among the dwelling houses in the city and suburbs. But since his time we have a great increase of glass-houses, founderies and sugar-bakers to add to the black catalogue; at the head of which must be placed the fire-engines of the water-works at London Bridge and York Buildings, which (whilst they are working) leave the astonished spectator at a loss to determine whether or not they tend to poison and destroy more of the inhabitants by their smoke and stench than they supply with their water. [Mr. Evelyn] also complains that the gardens about London would no longer bear fruit. It would now puzzle the most skillful gardener to keep fruit trees alive in these places; the complaint at this time would be, not that the trees were without fruit, but that they would not bear even leaves."

Mr. White then conceded that Evelyn's earlier plan to remove all manufacturing from London was no longer a practical possibility, thanks to a hundred years of industrial development. Still, if furnaces and kilns had to be permitted within the city, something should be done to limit their effect. He offered two proposals.

First, all commercial chimney stacks should be built high enough so that their smoke, soot, and gases would rise above the surrounding buildings and disperse into the atmosphere, instead of descending to the ground for people to breathe. Second, a method should be found to treat bituminous coal in such a way that all its smoke would be removed; only then would it be burned, industrially or in private dwellings, as a smokeless fuel. Although both proposals were of fundamental importance, they had to await the middle of our own century before business leaders and government officials would recognize the fact, and see to the implementation of these suggestions.

The author of the *Smoke of London* had ended on a note of optimism; Mr. White also chose to look hopefully into the future. John Evelyn, he wrote, "who had been very instrumental in restoring Charles to his Throne, was unfortunate in recommending a work of such consequence to so negligent and dissipated a patron. The [present] editor is encouraged by a more promising appearance of success. He has seen with pleasure many improvements of great importance to the elegance and welfare of this city undertaken and completed in a short time, when magistrates of less public spirit and perseverance than our present [ones] would have pronounced them impracticable."

Whether such admirable faith in municipal government, in Parliament, and in the king, was really justified, only the future would disclose. The question was a vital one, both for the citizens of London and for the inhabitants of many other important English towns.

By 1772, Great Britain had arrived at a turning. Changes were at hand that would utterly transform the appearance and the fabric of national life. A new age already had begun—the age of steam, iron, railroads, and ever-expanding business enterprise—an age that would be heavily dependent on the energy locked inside lumps of black, bituminous coal.

The last quarter of the eighteenth century was a time for restrictive measures; by acting with foresight then, it was still possible to ensure that the air of London—and of Britain's growing manufacturing centers—would remain at least reasonably endurable in the decades to come. But if the admonitions of White and Evelyn went unheeded, and if no steps were taken, then the future was plain. London, in 1772, already was smoky and sulfurous. It could only become infinitely more so, in the full tide of the Industrial Revolution.

Seven

IN MANY PARTS of Great Britain, life lost much of its rural character during the next seventy-five years. Even remote towns and villages became more accessible with the completion of a system of inland canals and waterways, the conversion of turnpikes from dirt to macadam, and the introduction of modern coal-burning railroads. A variety of new industries came into being; huge cotton mills sprang up in Lancashire; these, along with iron foundries and pottery works, all belching turbulent clouds of smoke from their low chimneys, soon gave the unwelcome name of "Black Country" to the shires of the West Midlands.

Within the space of four decades, iron production alone increased tenfold; to supply the new furnaces with fuel, thousands of men, women, and children were forced to leave their cottage industries to labor, instead, under appalling conditions, in the coal mines of Wales and the north.

Occupations were changing, too, in other sections of the country. Most Englishmen, in 1815, were still farm laborers or worked in trades closely allied to agriculture. Twenty years later, more than half the labor force was made up of townspeople who held jobs in industry. To house them, the nation's cities swelled enormously. Between 1800 and 1830, Manchester, Leeds, Liverpool, and Glasgow more than doubled in population, while Birmingham and Sheffield grew at an almost equal pace.

During this period of swift development and change, London enhanced her old-time importance. She was now the capital of the world's leading industrial nation and the center of a trading empire whose commercial sinews, reinforced by the power of the British Navy, extended around the globe.

Georgian London was also a dirty, unhealthy city, with

chronically polluted air. Coal now was burned by the ton rather than by the bushel, both in the capital itself and in the outlying suburbs. Old and new industrial plants daily hurled their smoke and gases into the atmosphere. Long-established factories still produced exquisite china and fine porcelain at Bow and Chelsea, but their chimneys were outnumbered by those of the huge, recently erected pottery works at Lambeth. Brickmaking was a growing source of pollution. The gas industry had gained a foothold in 1810 and was operating plants in Bermondsey, Greenwich, and Vauxhall. Printing machinery was manufactured in Finsbury and Southwark; clothing and furniture in the vicinity of Oxford Street and Piccadilly. Furnaces, factories, and workshops went up on sites convenient to the builder, with little or no regard to the dwellings in the neighborhood or to the air that the city's inhabitants would be forced to breathe.

Industrial chimneys were the most obvious source of pollution, but they were by no means the only one. More than a million people now made their homes within the city, and most of them used raw coal to heat and cook. They did so quite willingly, for the public's antipathy to the fuel from Newcastle had long since disappeared.

A nineteenth-century Londoner was accustomed to his smoky coal fire. He liked it. He was attached to it. For the poor, especially, the sight of the yellow flames dancing in the grate on a cold, damp night, was one of the few domestic pleasures in an otherwise drab, impoverished existence. And so, month after month, and year after year, with no awareness that they were undermining the health of their children, themselves, their neighbors, London's householders swept out the cinders and laid on a fresh supply of coal, lit their fires, and contentedly watched them burn. Their chimneys threw out tons of smoke and soot to darken the skies, to thicken and prolong the winter fogs, and to begrime and corrode the brick, stone, and metalwork of the city. But coal was cheap and warming, and there was no one to inform them of the harm they did or to suggest the benefits they would have derived from cleaner air.

Eventually, London grew so dark and smoky that its condition no longer could be entirely ignored. In 1819, for the first time since the reign of Elizabeth I, Parliament took official notice of the problem of atmospheric pollution. A Select Committee was appointed to study the question, with a view to the feasibility of constructing furnaces and steam-engines that would operate "in a manner less prejudicial to public health and comfort."

The committee set briskly about its task, and before many months announced its findings. Evidence taken from a number of experts made it clear that even in 1819 furnaces and stationary steam engines could be built in such a way that much of their smoke, soot, and assorted gases would either be greatly reduced or entirely eliminated. And yet no legislation followed. Indeed, it was to be another twenty-four years before Parliament even reopened the air pollution question.

Matters were not improved by the introduction of coal-burning railways into the city. The first line was opened in 1836; it carried passengers from London to Croydon and soon was extended to the resort city of Brighton on the coast. Other lines were quickly put into operation. One ran from Vauxhall to Southampton, another from London Bridge to Hastings, a third from Victoria to Margate, Deal, and Dover, with a spur to Greenwich, where the park was extremely popular with holiday crowds. These lines were principally suburban, and their smoke-filled marshaling yards, repair shops, and terminals lay just south of the Thames. Within a brief time after the main northern and western lines also had entered the city, London found itself a great railway hub, and its long-abused atmosphere was forced to absorb an additional burden of coal smoke and sulfur dioxide.

By the early 1840's something had to be done, and Parliament responded—with a new Select Committee. Hearings were held in 1843, and a report of the findings duly appeared. The committee recommended a bill "to deal with nuisances from furnaces and steam engines," and then concluded with the sanguine but baseless hope that "the same black smoke proceeding from fires in private dwellings, and all other places, may eventually be entirely prevented."

Two years later, in the absence of any legislation, yet another Select Committee was formed to have a fresh look at the problem. This time less optimism was expressed over the chances of improving London's air. For, the committee reported, "it is not to be expected in the present state of our knowledge that any law can be practically applied to the fire-places of common houses, which in a large town like London contribute very materially to the pollution of the atmosphere." Exactly why "the present state of our knowledge" was so inadequate, or whether it could be effectively extended during the immediate future, were questions not considered. It was far simpler to say that nothing could be done, and there to let the matter drop. By such proceedings, the 1845 committee provided an admirable model of apathy and indifference that would prove useful to manufacturers, engineers, municipal councillors, and parliamentary legislators for the next hundred years.

Not satisfied, however, with complete inaction, Parliament discovered an alternate route to the same end; it enacted a series of measures that for one reason or another could not be enforced. The Railway Consolidation Act of 1845 required "locomotives to be so constructed as to consume their own smoke." In the light of engineering knowledge of the time, this was a manifest impossibility. The Towns Improvement Act of 1847 contained a provision that new factory furnaces "be constructed to consume smoke arising from the fuel used" but provided no means for ensuring that the desirable provision would be obeyed. To rectify this oversight, Lord Palmerston's Acts of 1853 and 1856 empowered the police "to enforce provisions against smoke from furnaces used in steam raising, other furnaces employed in factories, public baths and washhouses, and furnaces used in the working of steam vessels on the Thames." Unfortunately, what constituted a nuisance was described so vaguely that the police rarely attempted to bring even the worst offenders to account.

By midcentury the smoke-laden fogs of London had become prodigious. The city's "pea-soupers" were now so thick, pervasive, and enveloping that they seemed to have an elemental life of their own and to be as much a true phenomenon of nature—which they were not—as an earthquake or a volcanic eruption. Since they were an accustomed burden, stoical Londoners accepted them, along with muddy winter streets and unsanitary drinking water, as an unpleasant but inevitable commonplace of life in their great, sprawling town.

Then a curious change occurred. The fogs of London were discovered by certain Victorian writers who described them in detail and ultimately turned them into a spurious romantic legend. One of the principal culprits was Charles Dickens, a fact as unlikely as it was ironic. When it came to child-abuse, unjust penal laws, or the dilatory conduct of the courts of chancery, the humane Dickens was always on the side of the angels. But when it came to filthy air, the same author could see only an opportunity to create a memorable literary effect or the chance to indulge in some harmless, good-natured whimsy.

Bleak House, published in 1852—almost exactly a hundred years before the advent of the great killer smog—gave the fogs of London an international reputation and a new name. The baptism occurred, as readers around the world soon learned, when the novel's heroine came to the city for the first time and was helped from her stagecoach by the enterprising Mr. Guppy:

> He [Mr. Guppy] was very obliging; and as he handed me into a fly, after superintending the removal of my boxes, I asked him whether there was a great fire anywhere? For the streets were so full of dense brown smoke that scarcely anything was to be seen.
>
> "O dear no, miss," he said. "This is a London particular."
>
> I had never heard of such a thing.
>
> "A fog, miss," said the young gentleman.

"London particular" or "pea-souper"—the poisoned fogs of the city were growing thicker, smokier, more dangerous. What was needed was not a new term to describe them, but a writer of Dickens' skill joining in a campaign of public enlightenment and protest. Unhappily, the great novelist's understanding lay elsewhere, and by the time he had finished describing the fogs of London in his unique style, they had become a world-famous institution of which a local citizen could be proud, rather than a crippling social evil he might wish to eradicate.

Eight

THE CAMPAIGN for air pollution control made little headway during the final decades of the nineteenth century. At first glance nothing could be stranger, for this was a period in Great Britain of zealous crusaders and noteworthy reforms. During the Victorian age, Edwin Chadwick helped to rid London of cholera by improving the city's water supply; Florence Nightingale established new sanitary standards for hospitals and created the modern nursing profession; Lord Shaftesbury saw to the passage of legislation which, if it did not entirely eliminate the evils of the sweatshop and child labor, at least did much to ameliorate the lot of the nation's most grievously exploited workers. Yet in the fight for cleaner air there were only a handful of hollow triumphs, with no prospect whatever of final victory.

The air pollution reformers of that era failed for many and varied reasons. Their program was difficult to promote and lacked immediate public appeal; its urgency was often questioned by some of the most important members of the community, who asserted—quite truthfully—that it was impossible to tell how many people died each year because of polluted air or, in numerous instances, who the victims were. Nor did the problem lend itself to a single, all-encompassing solution.

By contrast, it was a comparatively simple matter to rally the London populace against the threat of cholera. The disease was dramatic, its victims could be readily identified, and about half of those who fell ill died shortly afterward. More helpful still, the city's drinking water was known to be the single source of infection. Find new supplies of pure water, shut off the noxious cesspools that lay under many buildings, remove the offal, the raw sewage, the dead cats and dogs floating in ponds, streams, and sewers which sometimes were used as city reservoirs, and the disease could be brought expeditiously to an end.

But clean up the atmosphere of an entire city? Train four million people to burn coal more efficiently in their homes? Or supply them with a smokeless fuel—and persuade them to use it? Curb industrial smoke and wastes from the new electrical generating plants, the gasworks, the sugar refineries, the railway yards, the river's shipping? The complex task was truly formidable, and government, both national and local, shrank as long as possible from attempting it, especially in the absence of enthusiastic support from either the medical profession or the general public.

And then, standing in the way of reform, was the most insurmountable obstacle of all. Laissez-faire capitalists bluntly declared that dirty air was desirable; it meant profit for manufacturers, jobs for thousands of workers, and fiscal health for the country as a whole. According to the prevailing doctrine, clouds of smoke pouring from industrial chimney stacks were the reassuring visual expression of the nation's economic well-being. If cities like Manchester, Glasgow, and London were dirty and streaked with grime, and if far too many of their inhabitants suffered from such crippling diseases as chronic bronchitis and emphysema, this was the unhappy but necessary price that had to be paid for national prosperity. "Muck is money" became the popular slogan of those opposed to air pollution control, an opposition which said that to tamper with the system in any way would be to court economic disaster. Industrial wastes were not only essential, they were proper and respectable; in Victorian England, respectability was always a difficult antagonist to overcome.

Yet all the economic theories in the world could not disguise the fact that the atmosphere of London was in a truly appalling condition. For the first time, public health authorities were compiling meaningful weekly mortality statistics; these revealed that during the winter months, particularly when low temperatures coincided with spells of heavy fog, the death rate among Londoners increased enormously.

The winter of 1873-74 was a memorable one in London. The capital was plagued by persistent fogs from November through February, with only brief periods of intermittent sunlight to relieve the gloom. A heavy pea-souper descended on the ninth of December and did not lift until the twelfth. A week later the average for deaths had risen almost 75 percent, and three times the anticipated number of bronchitics lay dead and awaiting burial.

The smoke-polluted fog had killed hundreds, but it would be a mistake to believe that the event was followed by a tremendous outcry of public indignation. As one leading twentieth-century air pollution authority has written, "More concern was voiced over the fact that a cattle show was in progress at the time, and that many prize beasts were suffocated and others had to be put out of their misery."

Whether impelled by sympathy for human suffering or merely by an interest in prize cattle, two years later parliament approved the passage of the Public Health Act (1875), a piece of broad legislation which contained a section dealing with smoke abatement. At first, the advocates of air pollution control were greatly heartened; their joy diminished, as one by one a number of fatal loopholes were disclosed.

The most obvious was that no restrictions were placed on private dwellings, so that London's millions of domestic chimneys continued to pollute the air without restraint.

Then, under the Act, all commercial fireplaces and furnaces were expected to consume their own smoke "as far as practicable." But since it was almost impossible to determine legally what standard of efficiency was "practicable" for any given fireplace or chimney, this clause was of little value in curbing offenders.

Another clause in the Act prohibited chimneys from emitting black smoke in quantities sufficient to be considered a nuisance. But as sanitary inspectors soon discovered, it was a difficult feat to prove that last week's smoke had been "black" or that there had been enough of it to constitute a "nuisance" in the eyes of the law.

Finally, as a sop to business interests, all mining and smelting operations were specifically exempted from control and, by one legal device or another, so were most of the nation's other major industries. As for the owner of a plant which *had* been declared a smoke nuisance, the prospect of punishment was hardly terrifying. Twenty-five dollars was the maximum penalty for conviction, with the further possibility of an additional two dollars and fifty cents a day being levied if the offender failed to eliminate his nuisance quickly enough to satisfy the court. At such reasonable rates, the average capitalist had little reason to complain.

Atmospheric conditions in London did not improve. Between 1880 and 1892 at least four severe smoke-fogs—or smogs—occurred, each killing hundreds of local citizens. Victims for the most part were the elderly, especially those with a previous history of lung and chest complaints. Their deaths excited no great interest, for they had been anticipated by government medical authorities.

Meanwhile, at the close of the century, a new and final chapter in the legend of London's "glamorous" pea-soupers was being written. The world's most famous detective, Sherlock Holmes, was on the scene, battling against the criminal cunning of the London underworld—and doing it much of the time, Conan Doyle's readers came to believe, in the midst of swirling clouds of thick, yellow fog.

Nowhere did the author describe more vividly a London pea-souper than in his memorable story *The Bruce-Partington Plans*. As Dr. Watson related:

In the third week of November, in the year 1895, a dense yellow fog settled down upon London. From the Monday to the Thursday I doubt whether it was ever possible from our windows in Baker Street to see the loom of the opposite houses. The first day Holmes had spent in cross-indexing his huge book of references. The second and third had been patiently occupied upon a subject which he had recently made his hobby—the music of the Middle Ages. But when, for the fourth time, after pushing back our chairs from breakfast we saw the greasy, heavy brown swirl still drifting past us and condensing in oily drops upon the window-panes, my comrade's impatient and active nature could endure this drab existence no longer. He paced restlessly about our sitting-room in a fever of suppressed energy, biting his nails, tapping the furniture, and chafing against inaction.

"Nothing of interest in the paper, Watson?" he said.

I was aware that by anything of interest, Holmes meant anything of criminal interest. There was the news of a revolution, of a possible war, and of an impending change of government; but these did not come within the horizon of my companion. I could see nothing recorded in the shape of crime which was not commonplace and futile. Holmes groaned and resumed his restless meanderings.

"The London criminal is certainly a dull fellow," said he in the querulous voice of the sportsman whose game has failed him. "Look out of this window, Watson. See how the figures loom up, are dimly seen, and then blend once more into the cloud-bank. The thief or the murderer could roam London on such a day as the tiger does the jungle, unseen until he pounces, and then evident only to his victim."

"There have," said I, "been numerous petty thefts."

Holmes snorted his contempt.

"This great and sombre stage is set for something more worthy than that," said he. "It is fortunate for this community that I am not a criminal."

"It is, indeed!" said I heartily.

"Suppose that I were Brooks or Woodhouse, or any of the fifty men who have good reason for taking my life, how long could I survive against my own pursuit? A sum-

> mons, a bogus appointment, and all would be over. It is well they don't have days of fog in the Latin countries—the countries of assassination. By Jove! here comes something at last to break our dead monotony."

Holmes and Watson were fortunate that their fictional tedium could be so easily broken. For the ordinary citizens of London, especially those afflicted with chronic chest complaints, there was no relief from the "dead monotony" of cold, fog-laden winter air, irritated throats, a painful shortness of breath—and from the recurring dream of future sunlight and bright spring weather which, for some at least, did not always manage to arrive in time.

Nine

DURING THE FIRST decades of the present century, the grave and increasingly complex problem of polluted air was almost entirely ignored by British business leaders, politicians, and officials of the national government. In this they were abetted by widespread public apathy and by newspapers that frequently ridiculed any serious effort to promote reform.

The opposition to air pollution control was strong and entrenched. In many boroughs, when smoke or sanitary inspectors brought their complaints to court, the magistrates shielded the offending industrialists from even the mild penalties of the law. Under powers granted them by the Public Health Act, a handful of borough councils did achieve a modest amount of improvement, and some of the most intolerable cases of black-smoke emissions were finally curbed. In most instances, however, the Public Health Act was ineffective, and the improvements few and extremely limited.

Even the growing possibility of an air pollution disaster failed to cause concern. A few doctors, local public health officials, and meteorologists appreciated the danger and attempted, like Dr. Russell, a leading Glasgow expert, to warn others of the danger. "During the winter," the doctor wrote, "if certain weather conditions occurred—a combination of frost, fog, and still air for days together—every city [in Great Britain] would be in danger of a catastrophe." His words stirred little interest at the Ministry of Health, among legislators, or in the mind of the general public.

The ranks of the reformers were filled with earnest, humane, and well-intentioned citizens, but by any reasonable standard the progress they made was agonizingly slow. In extenuation, they had little money at their command and no particular gift for raising any; they lacked a popular cause, and they rarely found enthusiasm or even support at any level of government. In such circumstances, the reform movement needed the militant leadership of a Chadwick or a Shaftesbury or, perhaps, the single-minded fanaticism—and the genius—of a Florence Nightingale. Instead, the advocates of clean air were led by intelligent but conventional men who had no taste for drama or controversy and no desire to mount a forceful, imaginative campaign to capture the interest of the man-in-the-street. Sensationalism was to be avoided at all costs, and in this aim at least the reform movement was completely successful.

Lacking any sense of urgency, the reformers decided on a decorous policy of education, persuasion, and gradual change. Working through local smoke abatement societies, particularly those in London and Manchester, the advocates of clean air set out to influence "the informed and responsible minority—the creators of public opinion in Government circles, among local authorities, learned, technical and similar societies, writers and politicians."

To a very limited degree this sober strategy achieved worthwhile results. Significant innovations were made, such as the measurement of atmospheric pollution by specially designed instruments, the introduction of smokeless fuels, and the promotion of more efficient furnaces and fire grates for the burning of coal. Even more important, at least a small segment of the "informed and responsible minority" was indeed won over to the cause of clean air. But the trouble was that it all took too long. Time was not on the side of the reformers, a consideration that seemingly did not occur to them.

In 1905 a London physician, Dr. Harold Des Voeux, one of the most prominent leaders in the fight for smoke abatement, addressed a public health congress on the subject of polluted air. Dr. Des Voeux was a slight, spare man, with fair hair and spectacles, an engaging speaker who possessed a ready gift of phrase. Seeking to describe smoke-polluted fog to his audience, he created a term that would have instantly delighted any modern public relations expert—he coined the word "smog." But the reformers were not interested in a free-swinging publicity campaign and never employed the term to promote their crusade. When "smog" finally did come into common use in Great Britain—a half century later—it arrived by way of California and the Los Angeles freeway.

In London another little-noticed event also took place in 1905. At almost the same time that Dr. Des Voeux was addressing the public health congress, a small group of motorcar enthusiasts was banding together to form the Automobile Association. Even as the advocates of reform discussed fire grates and improved boiler operations, the internal combustion engine was preparing to add carbon monoxide, aldehydes, and half a dozen other brand-new pollutants to the witches' brew that was already London's air.

During the following years, Parliament and the national government procrastinated, pondered, and delayed. In 1913 a Smoke Abatement Bill was introduced in the House of Commons—unsuccessfully. A year later, Lord Newton, at the behest of a small number of local authorities, introduced a similar measure in the House of Lords. It was withdrawn on the understanding that Herbert Samuel, president of the Board of Trade, would set up "a strong departmental committee to examine the situation and make recommendations."

Such a committee was appointed in 1914, an unhappy bit of timing because its work was almost immediately suspended by the outbreak of the First World War. Not until six more years had passed was a new committee appointed, this time by the Minister of Health, under the chairmanship of Lord Newton.

In 1921 the Newton Committee published its *Final Report*. Privately, even the document's most ardent apologist must have been tempted to acknowledge that it was an extremely melancholy performance. And yet not everyone thought so. Nothing could indicate how befuddled the reformers were—or how abject their hopes. *They* interpreted the report as a minor triumph.

"The obvious conclusion to be drawn from our inquiry," the committee said, blandly confirming facts which had been recognized for well over fifty years, "is that the prevalence of smoke pollution in this country is due to the indiscriminate and wasteful use of raw coal for all purposes, whether industrial or domestic, and the lax administration of the law by the responsible authorities . . . perhaps the chief factor in the failure to deal with the smoke evil has been the inaction of the Central Authority. No Government has, for many years, taken any action with the exception of appointing committees, whose labors have led to little or no results. Smoke and air pollution are, in our opinion, a national question, and we consider it useless to expect that it will be adequately dealt with by local [borough] authorities unless they are subject, when necessary, to the stimulus of [national] Government. It is for this reason that we recommend that defaulting authorities should be compelled to act by the Minister of Health."

Here was the "triumph" of the reformers—assuming that a way could be found to compel the Minister of Health to perform his proper duties as they had never been performed in the past. Surely, then, one would have supposed, stringent new legislation would be recommended.

But the committee thought otherwise. Its report went on to say that "although amending legislation to a limited extent will be necessary, the chief requisite is the enforcement of the existing law." Grossly inadequate when passed in 1875, the old Public Health Act still seemed satisfactory to the Newton Committee members in 1921.

The nation's industrialists could hardly have been thrown into panic by some of the committee's other conclusions. One of these was the warm reassurance that business might go on as usual. "In the course of our investigations," the report stated, "we have never ceased to bear in mind that the interests of trade must be fully considered, and that the introduction of legislation which might prejudicially affect important industries is quite out of the question. We are convinced, however, that our recommendations are not calculated to inflict damage upon any industry; that they are of a practical nature, and that if adopted they will go far to increase the amenity of life in this country, and to modify, if not remove, an unsatisfactory state of things which is discreditable to a highly civilized community."

And there it was, a mere exercise in rhetoric to sugar-coat the old belief that "muck is money" and to disguise the unpalatable fact that unrestricted industrial pollution could still find its enthusiastic champions in the high places of government.

As for the other major problem—smoke from domestic chimneys—the committee examined the matter and then absolutely outdid itself. "The evidence clearly shows," the members wrote, "that a large percentage of the smoke in the atmosphere of towns comes from chimneys of dwelling houses . . . [and] as we have stated, there is today in this country, no law touching on the emission of domestic smoke, which is caused by the burning of raw coal."

Apparently the committee understood the need for such a vital and long-overdue law and was about to recommend that Parliament enact one. But the ways of governmental committees are sometimes strange, and little should be taken for granted about their proceedings. The *Final Report* continued: "The burning of raw coal is a dirty, wasteful and unscientific practice, and on the grounds of economy, as well as of public health, it should be restricted as much as possible, but, after full consideration, we do not consider it practicable at present to propose legislation dealing with smoke from private dwelling houses."

All that an unbiased observer could have said was "shades of the Select Committee of 1845!"

Scarcely a year later, as government paused again for further reflection, nature issued one of its sharp, periodic warnings. During November, 1922, heavy fog was experienced throughout many parts of the country. In London, the death rate from respiratory diseases more than doubled. The lethal properties of urban smog were now recognized, at least in some professional circles, as the medical correspondent of *The Times* disclosed in an article published soon after the smog had lifted.

"It will be seen," he wrote, "that in the foggy period November 12 to 25 the London death rate rose sharply above the rest of the country in general, and that this rise corresponded to the increase in the number of cases of bronchitis and broncho-pneumonia. There is at present no influenza epidemic, and consequently this rise may fairly be ascribed to weather conditions—to the darkness and irritation of the London fog.

"Here is surely a strong argument in favor of smoke abatement. The broncho-pneumonia cases are largely among children, the bronchitis cases largely among old people. Old and young, therefore, are being sacrificed to our criminal carelessness in this matter."

Parliament's response to intimations of criminal carelessness came four years later, with the passage of the Public Health, or Smoke Abatement Act, of 1926. Even as subsequently amended, it wasn't a great improvement over the old Act of 1875. Nothing was done to limit the smoke and soot pouring from domestic chimneys. Pollution was still generously tolerated from industrial stacks, including "black" smoke that was almost as difficult as ever to define legally. And once the Act had been passed, the Ministry of

Health refused to approve a single local bylaw which either would have curbed any smoke save the black variety or reduced some of the other noxious industrial emissions. Still, with all its defects, the reformers somehow managed to convince themselves that the new Act was better than nothing. Only it wasn't. Indeed, it was actually worse, because it gave the illusion that air pollution was being reduced, when in reality the atmosphere of Great Britain, and certainly of London, was becoming dirtier and potentially far more lethal than it had ever been before.

Ten

ANOTHER WARNING came in 1930. This time it was more spectacular. Across the English Channel, on the first of December, a thick and persistent fog settled over Belgium. Temperatures remained low, the air was still, and above the Meuse River a thermal inversion took place, trapping fog between the steep, narrow sides of the river valley.

A fifteen mile stretch of the Meuse was affected. Although the area contained small villages and farms, it was also heavily industrialized. Lining the floor of the valley were steel mills, power stations, glass factories, lime furnaces, and plants producing zinc, sulfuric acid, and artificial fertilizer. For four days their stacks pumped a variety of wastes into the atmosphere. On the third of December, thousands of people in the valley began to feel distress. They coughed in the dense smog, they vomited, they gasped for breath. On the fourth and fifth, before the smog finally dispersed, several hundred people were seriously ill, and sixty were dead.

The Meuse valley disaster created headlines around the world. An "ordinary" fog, it was said, didn't kill so swiftly, injure so violently, or mark its victims so plainly.

This fog was unique and unprecedented, and a mass of rumors began to circulate—of mysterious airplanes swooping over the valley, of a secret poison gas that had been dropped, of a factory accident with lethal fumes leaking out of a broken pipe and seeping across the valley floor, an invisible killer. Dr. J.B.S. Haldane of Cambridge, one of Britain's most eminent scientists, even suggested that the Meuse valley might have experienced an outbreak of bubonic plague.

The Belgian government immediately began an investigation, and within a short time the rumors were dispelled. There had been no mysterious airplane, no factory accident, no outbreak of plague. The Meuse valley had experienced an acute air pollution disaster—and nothing else.

Deaths for the period had risen to ten and a half times the expected rate. Casualties included the elderly and those who had suffered from a prior lung or heart condition. Both adults and children of every age were made severely ill. Primarily, all the victims experienced an intense irritation of the respiratory tract. No single pollutant was the agent of the disaster. More than thirty impurities were present in the smog; most of them, when found in sufficient quantity, were either extremely injurious to health or definitely poisonous. The investigation committee concluded with the assertion that the fatal irritant could not be absolutely determined, but that it had probably been a mixture of sulfur dioxide gas and sulfur trioxide aerosol.

For the future there was, of course, a bright side to the picture, as far as the residents of London were concerned. *Their* fogs, after all, were different. Although the London variety did contain a rich amount of sulfur dioxide and a considerable mixture of industrial pollutants, still, they were principally characterized by soot, carbon particles, and the smoke from raw coal. Therefore, a killer smog of the Meuse valley sort was hardly a possibility. And there was a reassuring geographical difference, too. The Meuse valley was narrow and lay between steep cliffs. The Thames was open, a broad saucer really—hardly in the strict sense of the word a valley at all.

Why worry then? And nobody did. Business leaders, doctors, Members of Parliament, the staff at the Ministry of Health, members of the press—all soon forgot, or chose to ignore, the lesson of the Meuse. And all refused to ask themselves the question: Did responsible government owe its citizens better protection against such an aggravated assault on their health and lives? Or the further, and even more disturbing question: Had modern industrial society now entered an era in which, because of rapid and ever-increasing technological developments, government might no longer be able to guarantee the daily health and safety of its citizens, even if it really cared to do so?

Eleven

BY THE EARLY 1930's, a growing sense of futility had spread through the ranks of the reformers. Despite their best efforts over the past three decades, despite their meetings, discussions, clean air exhibits, the problem of Great Britain's polluted atmosphere was no nearer a solution now than it had been at the turn of the century. The nation's cities were often smogbound, and not infrequently a winter's day in London could turn out to be a notably disagreeable experience.

In 1929 the advocates of clean air had joined together in a single organization, the National Smoke Abatement Society. Five years later, the Society's president, Dr. Harold Des Voeux—by this time a gray-haired gentleman in his early seventies—addressed the annual meeting, held in Glasgow. He reminded his audience that the previous winter in London had been exceptionally bad, and that the city's fogs had been reported as "the worst ever experienced, not perhaps from their density but from their frequency . . . seldom delaying traffic but depressing to a degree not previously known [because of] their darkness and foul smell."

Even more discouraging, Dr. Des Voeux pointed out, had been their futile attempts to win over the press. The previous summer the Society had held an important meeting to discuss the subject of smokeless fuels. The few newspaper accounts had been "scanty, short, curt and unenthusiastic."

Worst of all had been the failure of their ancient scheme to capture the "informed minority," and through these intelligent opinion-makers, to gain the support of the general population. On this crucial point the doctor had to confess total defeat.

"Surely," he said, "we have preached and preached until our brains are empty . . . and how many disciples have we procured? Even in this enthusiastic city how many of its million inhabitants care two straws whether the air is clean or dirty...? Where is the fault? Is it ours or theirs?

"We do not want to create alarm," he continued, "but we do want those who live in our cities to recognize that they live under unhealthy conditions conducive to maladies which not only cause discomfort and annoyance and temporary disablement, but dire diseases of a nature persistent enough finally to undermine strength and vitality and to lead to an untimely end. What will arouse the man in the street? For unless we can do this the fight will continue for another thirty years."

There may have been other answers to the doctor's question, but one, at least, was distressingly obvious: wide support for the cause of clean air would only come after a sufficient number of victims had died in sufficiently dramatic circumstances. Supply the nation with a tragedy that would dwarf the Meuse valley disaster, and fear and indignation would at last be aroused. To do so, all that would be required were patience, the passage of time, and the almost inevitable formation of an exceptionally prolonged and severe temperature inversion over one of Great Britain's polluted cities. After that, matters would take care of themselves.

Twelve

IMPERCEPTIBLY, year by year, London's atmosphere continued to become more heavily contaminated. A few responsible newspapers, without enthusiastically supporting control measures, at least felt the need to report conditions and to remind their readers, from time to time, what sort of air they were taking into their lungs. A typical item appeared in *The Sunday Times*, in November, 1937.

"Last Sunday's fog was the dirtiest of the season," the paper said. "According to official records a cubic section of Kensington's atmosphere measuring a hundred yards each way contained, at one time in the afternoon, 8 lbs. of assorted grime."

London's pollution was now so vast that it no longer could be considered an exclusively local affair. "During the night," the newspaper account continued, "a light southeasterly breeze sprang up and carried the suspended accumulation of impurity out over Middlesex, Hertfordshire and Buckinghamshire to beyond the Chiltern Hills, where much of it came to earth on Monday. In south Bedfordshire villages remote from any town, there was an oily black deposit on windows and water butts, and when housewives brought in their washing from the line they were dismayed to find it in a worse state than before they had begun to wash it." The last phenomenon was so familiar to the women of London that the mention of it must have extorted a weary smile from many a reader.

As bad as it already was, the air of the city was soon destined to grow even dirtier. Less than two years later the Second World War began, and by 1940 the Ministry of Home Security had evolved an ingenious scheme to conceal important targets from Nazi photoreconnaissance planes and bombers. Pollute the air, said the Ministry. Create additional smog, and do it deliberately. A departmental memorandum then was issued suspending all industrial smoke abatement activities. Following this, certain factories were ordered to produce as much smoke as possible from their chimneys, either by burning greater quantities of coal or by completely dismantling their control devices.

Eventually, however, the planners realized that this scheme was doing more harm than good. By 1943 a severe coal shortage had developed, and it did not seem a clever idea to continue wasting the precious fuel so wantonly. The Ministry of Fuel and Power issued a new directive, one that was heartily welcomed by the citizens of London and other British towns. "Industrial haze due to smoke from factories," the Ministry announced, "certainly makes it more difficult for enemy bombers to spot vital targets in industrial areas. But it cannot be stressed too strongly that the fuel situation demands that extra fuel should not at present be used for this purpose. The maximum amount of *work* for the minimum amount of coal is more than a defensive measure: it is one of the strongest weapons of attack. We can and will beat off the enemy with it. Black smoke is a sign of fuel waste."

Indeed, black smoke had always been a sign of fuel waste, a fact which the smoke abatement societies had vainly been attempting to convey to various national governments for the past forty years. Now, thanks to a wartime shortage, the fact had to be temporarily recognized. A smoky industrial plant was an inefficient one, and the black filth pouring from its stacks represented an extravagance the hard-pressed nation could ill afford. But the implications were not really encouraging for the future. After peace returned, old attitudes were likely to reemerge, and a program to control industrial air pollution would still be immensely hard to come by.

The prospect of eventually reducing smoke and sulfur dioxide from private chimneys was even dimmer. An Englishman's right to an open coal fire had become sacred. Coke or gas might provide an equal amount of warmth, but, it was said, they could not provide an equal amount of aesthetic pleasure or an atmosphere of agreeable, domestic comfort and sociability.

Even *The Times* of London, usually levelheaded and prosaic, could not resist an occasional flight of poetic fancy when describing the virtues of an open coal fire. A leading article, published just after the war's end, declared: "The real [coal] fire, like a good talker, changes and adapts its moods. Sometimes it roars with heartiness and then sinks for awhile into a glowing and restful silence. . . . Its variety makes it the perfect companion to the pensive who want to look dreamily at the pictures in the fire. Those pictures change incessantly, and one brisk stir with the poker can produce a whole new gallery in a different style of art; but no one can stare long and sentimentally at the barred symmetrical face of a gas fire."

It was now less than a decade before the advent of London's great killer smog—the worst air pollution disaster in history—in which at least half the lethal smoke and sulfur dioxide would be produced by ordinary domestic coal fires. A "perfect companion to the pensive," according to the nation's most respected newspaper. "A fatal companion," would have been the more accurate description.

Thirteen

In 1945, after six long years of conflict, a weary Britain faced the task of postwar rebuilding. Many difficult problems stood in the way of recovery. Coal and other fuels were still expensive and in short supply; their conservation remained a vital necessity. At the same time, thousands of new homes were needed to replace those destroyed by bomb and fire during the war. When built, however, such homes would require fuel, placing an additional strain on the nation's already limited supplies. With these considerations in mind, Minister of Fuel and Power Emanuel Shinwell appointed a committee in 1946, under the chairmanship of Sir Ernest Simon, "to consider and advise on the use of fuel . . . with special regard to the efficient use of fuel resources and to the prevention of atmospheric pollution."

The Simon Committee *Report* was published later in the same year. Its recommendations were far more enlightened and progressive than those of its predecessor, the 1921 Newton Committee. Gas, electricity, and various solid smokeless fuels, rather than bituminous coal, were to be employed in all new housing; older dwellings would continue to burn raw coal, but only in more efficient ways. Eventually, as alternative supplies increased, even these older dwellings would be converted to some kind of smokeless fuel, and the result would be a sharp reduction in atmospheric pollution.

As admirable as the plan was, it failed to emphasize the need for prompt action. Summing up their thoughts, the members wrote: "If the recommendations of our report are effectively carried out, domestic smoke will steadily decrease and virtually disappear in from 20 to 30 years. That means the abolition of half the smoke. . . . If, meanwhile, industrial smoke is tackled with more vigour, we are confident that the smoke nuisance can virtually be ended in from 20 to 30 years."

Assuming, then, that the committee report would lead to truly effective legislation—as no previous report had done before—by 1966, or perhaps 1976, the citizens of London might finally be able to enjoy a certain amount of clean, healthful air.

Even this slow pace, however, seemed too swift and rash to one member of the committee, Viscount Ridley. In dissent, he submitted a Memorandum of Reservations. It included a statement that Great Britain's air pollution problems were far more complicated than the other committee members apparently realized. "While I agree," the Viscount said, "on the desirability of abolishing smoke, I think that any legislation should at least be delayed until there is more widespread knowledge of modern methods of burning fuel, until public opinion has been further educated on the subject, and until there are adequate supplies of smokeless fuel and suitable appliances."

Viscount Ridley's opinion prevailed. The recommendations of the majority were discounted, no vigorous and significant legislation followed, and the labors of still another special committee came to nothing.

Fourteen

AN UNRESPONSIVE government failed, in 1948, to heed a final, vivid warning of the dangers to be found in polluted air. Toward the end of October a temperature inversion occurred over a wide portion of the northeastern United States. Considerable fog formed along the Monongahela River, particularly in the town of Donora, about thirty miles south of Pittsburgh. The heavily industrialized community contained, among other works, a large steel mill and an equally important zinc reduction plant. The twisting river valley was narrow and, like the Meuse, lay between steep sloping cliffs.

Soon the natural fog in Donora had become a heavily contaminated smog. Observers noted an eerie sight; instead of rising in a natural way, the smoke from factories and railroad engines, trapped by the still, cold air, was spilling to the ground. In time the people of Donora began to cough and vomit and to experience difficulty in breathing. The smog lasted four days, before a cleansing rain dispelled it. By then, 17 excess deaths had been recorded and more than 40 percent of the ten thousand inhabitants had been made ill.

Local authorities called on the federal government for aid, and the United States Public Health Service conducted a prompt and searching investigation. Its well-documented conclusions were read by public health officials and meteorologists around the world. Donora, Pennsylvania, had suffered an acute air pollution disaster quite similar to the Meuse valley disaster of 1930. Illness and death had come swiftly; those killed had been middle-aged or elderly people, with a preexisting heart or lung condition. Again, as in the Meuse valley disaster, the blame could not be placed on a single pollutant. Several had been present in significant quantities and were regarded with suspicion. They included the familiar sulfur oxides, and a variety of grits, fly ash, and soots, called collectively "particulate matter."

In November, while the Donora episode was still being studied, London suffered a smog disaster of its own. The event received little attention because the British government, the press, and the people themselves were reconciled to what they supposed was an inevitable loss of life through an occasional pea-souper.

Although at least three hundred people died in the London smog of 1948—more than 17 times the number killed in Donora—the Ministry of Health was not called upon to conduct an extensive investigation. The city's regular mortality records clearly revealed that the majority of the victims had been either elderly bronchitics or emphysema patients, as any competent medical authority could have predicted. The dead had been "hanging on the edge," and according to the official view, soon would have slipped over anyway. If not during one smog, then during the next, or the next. And really—when one thought about it rationally—did it make a great deal of difference if a handful of the elderly sick were pushed into their graves a few months or even a few years before their time? Of course that *would* sound a bit cynical to certain high-minded idealists who liked to stir up a fuss, so it might be better to express one's opinions discreetly.

Fifteen

THE MONTHS slipped quietly away, while the government failed to offer effective legislation and its various ministries failed to use their existing powers to deal with the air pollution problem. Sporadic protests continued to be made against bureaucratic inaction. At a public conference in 1949, James Law, Sanitary Inspector for Sheffield and Rotherham, recited the particulars of what, by now, was an old, old story.

One should have expected, Mr. Law said, that the government, and particularly the Ministry of Health, would have been the principal advocates of clean air—but they were not. When applications were made by local authorities to the Ministry to obtain black-smoke bylaws, the applications were invariably refused. When a declaration of a national fuel policy was requested, the Ministry of Fuel and Power refused to declare one, stating, instead, that the people should have the freedom to choose the types of fuel they wished to use—and to contaminate, apparently forever, the air their helpless fellow citizens would be forced to breathe.

At a time, Mr. Law said, when air pollution in Great Britain was reaching new peaks of intensity, the Ministry of Fuel and Power was urging, not that factories employ better-grade fuels with a smaller sulfur content and less solid impurities, but lower-grade fuels that deposited vastly greater amounts of both sulfur oxides and particulate matter over wide residential areas. Indeed, the speaker had only recently received a visit from the same Ministry's Regional Fuel Engineer who had inspected a local factory and insisted that it immediately begin using lower-grade fuels, vetoing any alternative which might have spared the adjacent neighborhood an additional amount of pollution.

Several years before, Mr. Law concluded, new smoke

legislation had been drafted, subsequently approved at an air pollution conference, and finally forwarded to the Ministry of Health for its observations. Eighteen months had passed since then. It was understood that as yet, there had been no reply from the Ministry.

Sixteen

THE NEED for government action was even more pressing in 1952 than it had been ten, fifty, or a hundred years before. At last, remorselessly harried by a small but dedicated company of sanitary inspectors, smoke abatement advocates, news reporters, and local Medical Officers of Health, the government responded—with a new departmental committee. Its main purpose was to analyze the continuing fuel crisis; naturally, the question of polluted air would be examined and discussed. But the outlook for immediate and effective legislation did not seem bright. The chairman of the new committee was Viscount Ridley, who six years before had found the Simon Committee's *Report* too extreme.

During the autumn of 1952, Mr. Edward Davies, Member of Parliament from Stoke-on-Trent, North, submitted a question to the Minister of Housing and Local Government, the future Prime Minister, Mr. Harold Macmillan. The Member asked whether the Minister was satisfied that local authorities had adequate powers to deal with the industrial smoke nuisances in their localities, and whether he would take steps to strengthen those powers to assist them in their fight for a cleaner atmosphere.

Mr. Macmillan responded with a written reply. "Local authorities," he said, "have wide powers for the prevention of smoke nuisances under the Public Health Act . . . and while I am anxious to assist, I do not think that further legislation is necessary at present."

The reply was received on the twenty-first of October, six weeks before the onset of the great killer smog.

A fortnight or so later, subscribers to *The Evening News* might have paused uneasily and wondered what lay ahead of them had they bothered to read a feature article titled: "The Menace of Smog."

"Stand on the heights of Hampstead or Blackheath," the article said, ". . . and it will be seen that the gray dome of St. Paul's stands above a layer of mist stretching from the cranes and derricks of the Pool to the gasometers of West London.

"That layer is smog, an urban combination of smoke and fog. It is not only smoke particles, but also an almost infinite variety of chemical compounds, in solid, liquid and gaseous form.

"In that air are varying amounts of soot, ash, carbon monoxide, sulfur dioxide, oxides of nitrogen, hydro-carbons, organic acids, methane, acetylene, phenols, ketones, ammonia, alcohols and much else besides—a veritable chemical storehouse.

"Last week the director of the Fuel Research Laboratory at Greenwich announced that *despite* the installation of gas removers at Battersea and Fulham power stations the concentration of sulfur dioxide in the air over Westminster, Chelsea, Wandsworth, Battersea and Lambeth is now much what it was before."

The paper's readers might also have pondered this prophetic addition: "Smog is always with us, as we shall probably learn this month."

And so, November ended and December began. Greater London, an unsuspecting city of eight-and-a-quarter-million people, lay squarely in the path of a huge mass of cold, dry air, now inching slowly eastward across the open ocean.

The warnings, pleas, exhortations of many decades—even of centuries—had all passed unheeded. The beginning of the great killer smog was less than a hundred hours away.

Part Two—Anatomy of a Disaster

"Not until the death certificates were assembled and analysed did the extent of the excessive mortality become apparent. . . . It must in truth be a supreme example of the way in which a Metropolis of eight and a quarter million people can experience a disaster of this size without being conscious all the while of its occurrence."

Ministry of Health,
REPORT NO. 95., January, 1954.

Chapter Seventeen

THE WEEK OF the smog began with deceptively pleasant weather. On Monday, December 1, London experienced normal winter temperatures; the winds were light to brisk, the air clear, and there was a good deal of sunlight.

Most of the city's millions occupied themselves as they ordinarily did. Before sunup they lit their coal fires to take away some of the chill; housewives made breakfast; husbands left for work; tardy children raced down the street to school.

During the day, Londoners shopped, worked at a thousand different tasks, and then returned home by Underground, bus, or suburban train. In spare moments they read a newspaper, critically surveyed the garden, or listened to the BBC. Some arranged weekend plans that would have to be postponed. Others arranged weekend plans that would never be fulfilled.

Millions of Londoners worked and ate, quarreled or made love, took up a new hobby, planned a crime, or went to the cinema—those who would live only a few days longer, those who would fall sick and then recover, those who would find the great killer smog no more than an inconvenience and remember it afterward for some unusual incident in which they had been involved, or merely for a single, vivid impression. All mingling together, talking, forming queues, passing one another on the street or along an office corridor—and none aware of what was to come, or of the invisible mark that already was on a relative, a friend, a neighbor.

Save for the approaching Christmas holidays, there was no special excitement. Certainly there was no hint of danger, of threatening calamity. London, like any other modern Western city—New York, Los Angeles, Chicago—believed itself immune to disaster.

For plump and sociable Mrs. Wilcox, Monday, December 1, proved a cheerful day. She had long been awaiting news from her husband, and a letter finally arrived in the morning mail bearing a Singapore postmark.

Derek Wilcox worked for the P & O Line as a chief purser. His letter, which she opened at once, began by confirming something she had been counting on—that Mr. Wilcox would be home the week of the twentieth, in ample time for Christmas.

She continued to read the letter while sitting in a folding chair in the sunny back-garden of their small, two-story suburban home. The Wilcoxes were childless. They lived in South Norwood, near Croydon, about ten miles south of central London. It was flat country and not to everyone's taste. Mrs. Wilcox liked it, though, for she had lived in the area most of her life and was used to it.

And their back-garden really was very pretty. It didn't appear at its best now, of course, not so late in the year.

There were only a few roses left and some rather weary-looking snapdragons. But the leaves of the holly tree were green and shiny, and Mr. Wilcox would be glad to see the tree again. He was always glad to see it after one of his voyages. Thinking of the holly brought Christmas to mind, and she decided that on Friday afternoon, when she had finished her housework, she would close up the place and go in to Croydon for an hour or two to buy some Christmas gifts.

The letter from Singapore went on for several pages. At the end it cautioned Mrs. Wilcox, who was 53, to take care of her health. "When you get too excited, or overdo," her husband had written, "it brings on the migraine." Mrs. Wilcox needed no reminder. Once or twice each year she experienced a blinding headache that left her feeling exhausted for hours or even days afterward.

The letter did not mention her other complaint. Esther Wilcox suffered from chronic bronchitis. Her condition was moderately well advanced.

At a school in north London, Angela Burke spent most of Monday thinking about her hair. She was almost seventeen, and the only girl over fourteen who still had to wear her hair in braids. That's why they'd had another fight the night before—she and her mother.

All they ever seemed to do anymore was fight. Most of the time it was about the same thing—whether or not she was still too young to have her hair cut short. Her mother just wanted to keep her a child forever. Well, she was tired of being treated like one. And her dad wasn't any help, either. All he ever did was to hide behind his newspaper and say, "Why don't you wait a little bit longer, Angie? Maybe a few weeks more, and your mother will tell you it's all right."

She knew better. Her mother never would say it was all right. So she wouldn't argue with her anymore; she'd just take the money she had saved and go to the hairdressers, *that's* what she'd do. First have it cut and then waved, and after that her mother could say anything she liked—the braids would be gone.

Angela Burke squared her jaw. A glimpse at her reflection in the window told her that it didn't make her look any prettier, but she didn't care—she didn't care about anything except having her hair cut short.

She would go to the hairdressers over the weekend, when there wasn't any school. Angela Burke decided to have it done on Saturday morning.

Dr. Charles White knew that he should not have remained in Knightsbridge so late in the season. He was 67, a widower, and a former Medical Officer of Health. After more than twenty years' service in one of the metropolitan boroughs, he was quite familiar with the effects that a London fog could have on someone in precarious health.

Ordinarily he would have been gone from the city long before this. Each year since the war it had been his custom to leave England in late October, cross France by train, and then take the boat to Egypt to spend the winter months in the warm, benign climate of the Nile valley. It was a regime he'd been following from the time when declining health—bronchitis, complicated by emphysema and arteriosclerotic heart disease—had forced him into an early retirement.

This year, though, he hadn't been able to follow his normal schedule. Early in October his youngest sister had had a mishap. She'd caught her heel on a rug, fallen, and broken her hip. All his life he had acted as head of the family, and now he found that he wasn't particularly keen on giving up the role. Instead of departing for Egypt and leaving his brother-in-law in charge of things at home, he decided to stay on, just for an extra fortnight or two, until he could be certain that his sister was properly on the mend.

But in late October he had caught a heavy cold; there was a persistent cough; the cold turned into pneumonia. A stay in hospital, administration of penicillin, bed rest—the lot—had done the trick. Now he was on his pins again. A trifle shaky, but eager to be off to the south the following week.

Dr. White spent a quiet Monday in his Knightsbridge flat, only a few steps from Hyde Park. He talked with his sister on the telephone and promised to visit her Friday. By then he'd be fit enough to be getting around. He also arranged to have dinner Saturday evening with his nephew.

For the rest of the day he napped and leafed through some books about Egypt. It was amazing how the exceptionally dry air in that country had helped to preserve certain mortuary artifacts for twenty-five centuries and longer.

When he thought about London's weather, he did so with a quick shrug. One needed a bit of luck, that was all. Any medical textbook could have told you, "It is desirable for the bronchitic to live in a mild, equable climate, especially during the winter months. . . ."

Let the weather remain just decently passable for another week, and he would be all right. Seven or eight more days, and he'd be off to the south.

Of course in the meantime he was running a risk, but he hadn't really had any choice in the matter. As head of the family, he had long since been compelled to assume certain extra responsibilities. In life, there were inescapable family obligations. And so, despite his own better judgment, here he was, still in Knightsbridge, on the first of December.

After six months in London, Jerry Briggs was getting used to the place. An American newspaperman, he shuttled each day between the wire service offices off Fleet Street and a spacious basement apartment in Hampstead, where he and his wife Dorothy had settled during the summer.

All in all, he was glad to be in London. Whatever you might say against it—damp climate, not enough ice in your drinks, the high price of cigarettes—the city was still a big improvement over his last two assignments, Karachi and Seoul.

Of course they did say the English winters could be pretty bad. He had never been in England during the wintertime. He had never been in a London pea-souper. Still, he wouldn't be too disappointed if they went ahead and decided to have one while he was here—might as well see what the natives have to put up with, as he'd said to Dot.

He didn't think of the weather, though, on Monday evening. A more important item was on his mind. When he got back to their place in Hampstead, he tried to be particularly good-humored about it. He could see that Dot was making a similar effort. In fact, neither of them spoke about her sister Ethel until after dinner. By then the kids were both in bed.

The news wasn't good. She was coming, all right. With her friend. Arriving on Thursday afternoon planning to stay with them in Hampstead through Saturday morning. Then the two "girls" would be off to Switzerland for the main part of their vacation.

Forty-eight hours with Ethel. He might survive—just barely.

For the tenth time that day, Jerry Briggs asked himself how two sisters could be so different. After all, they'd had the same parents, the same upbringing, the same everything. Dotty was really as good as gold. She had her faults, sure—who didn't? He probably had one or two himself. But she didn't get her nose out of joint if you happened to get slightly plastered and began flavoring the conversation with a few choice four-letter words.

Well, you just had to look at the bright side, that was all. On Thursday, Ethel and her chum would be tired out after their flight, so once dinner was over they'd probably be willing to go to bed early. Most of Friday he'd be working, thank God, and wouldn't have to see them. And Dot could take them around sight-seeing and wear them out some more. Saturday, right after lunch, he'd drive them to the airport to make sure they didn't miss the plane. Things would work out. Ethel was okay in small doses, say forty-eight hours or less.

Monday evening was a long, weary time for the Chapmans. They sat in the small row house in Hammersmith and talked about the baby, while trying to soothe and comfort him and lull him to sleep. Albert Chapman was four months old. Most of his brief life he had been sick.

In hospital, on that warm July day when the nurse had first brought the baby to her, he had seemed quite perfect, Mary Chapman remembered. Later, they had told her that he weighed seven pounds, seven ounces. A healthy baby. A son for John.

He wasn't a healthy baby, though. He caught colds so easily, and then he'd begin to cough. Looking at him, you would have thought he was entirely well, but just as soon as you heard how wheezy his breathing sounded, you would have known that there was something wrong.

The doctor had asked if there was any history of asthma in John's family or in hers. In John's, she'd said. Both his mother and grandmother had suffered from asthma for years. John thought his grandmother had died of it after an attack.

A marked asthmatic tendency, the doctor had assured her, was not uncommon in children. It caused a bit of difficulty while the child was still very young but, later on, Albert would outgrow the worst effects, and even now there was no reason to be gravely concerned.

The house in Hammersmith *was* too damp for the baby. She was certain of it. In September, when he'd caught a very bad cold, she'd taken him for a few days to her parents' house just off Watling Street in Little Stanmore, in the northern part of London. It was drier there. After a few days his breathing had grown easier, so she'd brought him back to Hammersmith again. For awhile he'd been all right.

Then, the last week in November, he'd caught still another cold. The doctor had *said* that any extra dampness in the Hammersmith house hadn't made any difference, but how could she really be sure?

The Chapmans talked the problem over as she rocked the baby. Finally, the medicine must have soothed him. Worn out with crying, Albert fell asleep.

They decided, before putting out their own light, that they would try the house in Little Stanmore again for a few days. And by next spring Albert would be almost a year old and much stronger. Everything would be better then.

Tomorrow she would take the baby to her parents', where it wasn't so damp. Mary Chapman felt a great sense of relief as she thought about it.

In London's great web of streets and houses, Monday, the first of December, finally came to an end. The city had enjoyed very good weather most of the day. Slight frost had been recorded in the morning; winds had been out of the north and east at 8 to 14 knots; mean air temperature had been a pleasant 36.9 degrees. Visibility had been excellent, from just under a mile to ten miles, at both Kew Observatory in the west and the Air Ministry Building at Kingsway in the heart of town.

The lights had gone out in the offices and laboratories at County Hall, the administrative center of the city, on the south bank of the Thames. Instruments there had recorded their measurements of atmospheric deposits. Sulfur dioxide was .09 parts per million, black matter .3 milligrams per cubic meter of smoke. Both figures were well within the normal range.

During the day district nurses in London County had begun home treatment of 81 new respiratory cases, an unexceptional number for a 24-hour period in December; 259 deaths, from all causes, had occurred in Greater London.

The London Ambulance Service, with headquarters near County Hall, had answered 261 calls. The ambulances had been out an average of 44 minutes, from station to hospital and back to station again.

There was no epidemic in the county, no outbreak of disease. London slept peacefully after a routine winter's day.

Eighteen

THE WEATHER remained quite pleasant in the city on Tuesday, December 2. Temperatures were slightly lower than on the previous day, but the air was still fresh, and for the time of year, there was a considerable amount of sunlight.

In central London all was bustle and haste, while in the suburbs life seemed to move at a more leisurely tempo. Mrs. Wilcox, in South Norwood, received another letter from her absent husband. At first she frowned when she saw that it had been written a full week before the one that had been delivered the previous day. *Really*, there was no accounting for the vagaries of the postal service.

But the letter cheered her up a good deal, all the same. Sometimes—especially when Mr. Wilcox had been away on one of his voyages for several weeks—she would begin to feel a bit lonely and forlorn, from being by herself in the house so much of the time. News from Mr. Wilcox, though, always put her in a better frame of mind. That—and thinking about the day when he'd return.

In Knightsbridge, Dr. White remained indoors on Tuesday. He had determined to give himself another day's rest. The truth was . . . he still didn't feel entirely up to snuff.

A lingering cough, skin rather pale, purulent phlegm, a faintly bluish tinge to the lips—rather more pronounced than on the previous day. Rest the heart for awhile yet. It was the only thing to do.

He settled down with a new book about the Valley of the Kings in Egypt—the lonely, hidden, treeless valley among the steep rock cliffs, where for almost three hundred years some of the most powerful of the ancient pharaohs had been secretly buried in their golden coffins and their splendid jewels.

He could almost feel the desert heat on his limbs. He could almost imagine himself there already.

Jerry Briggs was too busy most of the day to think about the imminent arrival of his sister-in-law. Major news stories were in short supply just then, and he had to do a bit of scrounging. . . . Prime Minister Winston Churchill had celebrated his seventy-eighth birthday on the first of the month and he had duly filed a detailed account, but that wasn't doing him much good today. . . . One possibility was the approaching coronation of the young queen. What route would Elizabeth II take and, more important, what would she be wearing?

There weren't too many other prospects. During the coming weekend the high commissioners of the Commonwealth countries would hold a reception in the still-damaged Guildhall. The fete might be of absorbing interest to British readers, but it wasn't likely to set a lot of Americans on fire. There was a major trial just getting underway at the Stafford Assizes. The case involved a rich widow and her alleged murderer, the young family chauffeur. He'd have to keep an eye on it, but the advance word was that nothing very spicy or sensational was likely to result.

Jerry Briggs decided to settle for the coronation. He only hoped he could come up with a worthwhile angle.

Early in the afternoon, Mary Chapman's mother arrived from Little Stanmore to help her move. They gathered together the baby's things, and then Mary packed a small suitcase for herself. Finally she and her mother took the baby in a taxi from Hammersmith to the house near Watling Street.

It really *was* much drier in her parents' house. She could tell that it was. Even after only an hour or two, by the time she and Albert were all settled in, his cough seemed to be growing better. A few days at her parents' were sure to benefit him, no matter what the doctor said.

When John telephoned that afternoon, she was much more cheerful than she had been the day before. And she reminded herself to be particularly nice to him that evening when he came to Little Stanmore on his way back from work. John, naturally enough, disliked being left alone in Hammersmith. She would point out to him, though, that the separation was only for a few days, and couldn't be helped, and that she and Albert would be back home with him, very, very soon.

A few miles from Little Stanmore, on the south side of the Thames, an unusual patient called at Dr. Geoffrey Roberts' dispensary. The man was a neighbor named Duncan Hunter. His visit made a deep impression. Five days later, during the worst of the weekend, the young doctor still remembered it vividly, and the recollection resulted in one of the strangest adventures that anyone experienced during the great killer smog.

Dr. Roberts was seated at his desk on Tuesday afternoon when the door opened. Looking up, he saw that Hunter, a blind man, had entered the office. Before he could rise and offer to help, Hunter already was halfway to the desk, guiding himself to a chair with the aid of his cane.

The self-assurance of the blind man was remarkable. After all, these quarters were not a part of his familiar surroundings. As far as Dr. Roberts could recall, the patient had only been in his office two or three times, and the last visit must have been many months before.

The doctor watched as Hunter made his way unhesitatingly to the chair by the desk. Apparently he had committed all the essential geography of the room to memory a long while past, and now, at a moment's notice, he could summon up every feature of the place. It was truly something to think about—the fantastically elastic limits of the human brain, limits that sometimes were only approached when one of the vital senses was destroyed and a different talent or ability, hitherto almost entirely latent, had to be called into service.

The blind man's complaint was simply stated. There was a small lump on his back. He'd had it for a few weeks, and now his wife had begun to nag at him to come round so the doctor could have a look.

After a brief examination Dr. Roberts told him the condition was no cause for concern. It was merely a benign cyst located above the left shoulder blade. He removed it without difficulty and put on a dressing. Hunter slipped into shirt and coat, thanked him, and guided himself expertly out of the room.

His curiosity aroused, Dr. Roberts consulted the files. He had *not* been mistaken. Duncan Hunter had visited his office only twice previously. The first time had been in 1949. The second had been in May of 1951—18 months before.

And yet, after only these two visits, the blind man possessed a perfect map of door, desk, chair—the entire office. Dr. Roberts shook his head. He found the performance absolutely astonishing.

"Healthy and fit" was the way that Michael Watts would have described himself. At 44 he was still a lean, trim, active six-footer, who loved to be out in the open air. His job as groundsman for one of the city's major football clubs was perfect for a man of his interests and temperament. He'd been an athletic youngster and that perhaps was why he now enjoyed being a part of the sports world, even if his role in it was only a small one. Whatever the reason, he found that keeping the turf in top condition for the team's home matches gave him a considerable amount of satisfaction. And there was a match scheduled for Saturday afternoon, the sixth of December.

Watts was out on the football pitch most of Tuesday. When quitting time came he slipped into his jacket, and after a last glance at the green field, headed off downhill for the bus stop. He walked with a light, agile step, enjoying the cool air. A flash of color down the road caught his eye. The bus was coming around the bend, one of London's handsome, red, double-deckers. If he hurried, he might just be able to catch it at the stop.

He broke into a long, easy lope, running gracefully, covering the ground with surprising speed. For a moment, though, he thought he'd misjudged the distance. The last person in the queue was just stepping aboard, and the bus was starting up by the time he came to the stop. Without breaking stride he sprinted forward and leaped into the back. He wasn't even breathing hard as he began to climb the stairs to the upper deck.

There was no way of knowing how many people in Greater London were as fit as Michael Watts. He had been given a clean bill of health the last time he'd been examined. He had never had any trouble with his lungs, neither as a child nor in recent years. No trouble whatever. It seemed unlikely that such a man could be affected even by an unusually dense and prolonged pea-souper.

Had you suggested the possibility to the appropriate health authorities or to the many able doctors practicing in the borough where Watts lived, you undoubtedly would have been told that you were being a damn fool, although the rebuke might have been phrased more politely. For it was perfectly well known that even the city's worst fogs struck at only the old, the infirm, and the very young—infants under the age of one or two. Certainly active adults, and anyone else in normal good health, were immune to danger.

Tuesday, December 2, had proved to be another unexceptional day. There had been a trace of frost in the morning, a touch of haze in the afternoon. Winds remained light to moderate, varying between 2 and 7 knots. Visibility was generally good, up to a mile at Kingsway and up to 3 miles at Kew.

During the 24-hour period, there had been no evidence of epidemic disease in the metropolis, and various health facilities were placed under no strain. The Ambulance Service answered 215 calls, and the clean, well-tended vehicles were out on each trip an average of 35 minutes.

The volume of smoke and sulfur dioxide in the atmosphere was greater than on Monday, but the increase was too small to be considered significant. No one could say how much additional air pollution there might have been, for only smoke and sulfur dioxide were measured each day. Not a single station in Greater London took a daily reading of any other gas or chemical, and less than a half-dozen stations even took such readings as often as once a month.

The lack of this sort of information did not seem to be of importance on Tuesday night. The past 24 hours had been quiet and untroubled, and the first month of the winter gave every indication of "coming in like a lamb."

Nineteen

WEDNESDAY, the third of December, was the finest day of the week. The atmosphere was clear and refreshing, the skies a dazzling blue, the city's streets and parks filled with warmth and sunlight. White, puffy, cumulous clouds drifted overhead. Northeast winds, a trifle stronger than on Monday, signaled the approach of a new weather system—a mass of cold, dry, slow-moving air, whose center was located several hundred miles to the west and north of the capital. Few people would remember it afterward, but London was a truly splendid place to be, on Wednesday, the third.

In South Norwood, Mrs. Wilcox was greatly cheered by the weather. At first, while eating a solitary breakfast in the kitchen, she had badly felt the want of company, but before long the morning became so warm and bright that her mood of depression soon passed. She spent part of the day at household chores, and after lunch, she sat for an hour in the garden behind the house, enjoying the air and the sunlight.

At teatime, a telephone call from her niece Amy left Mrs. Wilcox in an even better frame of mind. Amy was just moving with her husband and four-week-old baby into a new flat. Once they were settled, she would bring the baby around for a visit. The prospect was one that Mrs. Wilcox could look forward to. She told Amy to be sure and telephone, and in the meantime if there was anything *she* could do to help them, Amy was to let her know.

Off Fleet Street, Jerry Briggs resisted the blandishments of the weather and remained sunk in gloom. From time to time he made a fitful effort to deal with the current story of Sir Gerald Templer and the Malayan guerrilla campaign, but his heart just wasn't in it.

In less than 24 hours Ethel and her friend would be reaching London Airport, and he'd be there at Heathrow—the welcoming committee—ready to haul their bags to the car and then on to Hampstead. For a few idle and lovely moments he wondered whether a London-bound plane had ever landed in Rome by mistake, but it wasn't a fantasy with much life in it. The plain fact was that Ethel was coming, and there was no escape. He made a mental note to buy a couple of extra bottles of whiskey on the way home, then returned with a sigh to Sir Gerald and the guerrillas.

The day was so fine in Little Stanmore that Mary Chapman took Albert out in his pram both morning and afternoon.

The baby was so much better now and that's all that mattered. His cough had almost disappeared. His cheeks looked rosier. His breathing was easier, and there was hardly any wheeze.

She could scarcely wait for John to come back from work so that he could see the improvement for himself. They had never discussed it, naturally, but she was sure he felt guilty about the baby, because—though clearly he wasn't in the least to blame—the asthmatic tendency was all in his family. So now that Albert was better, it would be something off his mind.

Angela Burke was so upset that she hardly even noticed it was a beautiful day. Her mother had done it to her the first thing in the morning—deliberately. Instead of nattering on as she usually did about how cheap-looking the young girls were these days, she'd started in, without any warning, talking about God.

Saying to her father, right there at the breakfast table—though really saying it to *her*, of course—how a disobedient child was as cruel a thing to her parents as the bite of a serpent's tooth, or some such rot, and how God cast out from His sight any child who defied her parents' wishes, and how such a willful, disobedient child was *lost* to God and would surely feel the full weight of His wrath before very long. And on and on. She knew perfectly well why her mother was saying it, but the trouble was—she did believe in God *and what if her mother was right?*

The idea of God's wrath, of His awful punishment being visited upon her, haunted her entire day. She couldn't drive it out of her mind. It almost made her give up her plans—but not quite.

Across Rotten Row to Hyde Park, then on as far as the Serpentine, a slow walk by the water with frequent rests along the way, and finally an equally slow walk back home—that was the course Dr. White followed on his first day out of the flat in Knightsbridge.

Later, he called Thomas Cook and inquired about his reservations. He was told that the new tickets would be mailed to him that afternoon or the following morning. They would reach him no later than Friday. Train, ship, and hotel in Cairo—everything had been confirmed.

His cough did persist, despite the fine weather, but there was no question that he felt better than he had in weeks.

In the middle of a sunny afternoon in Stepney, young Mrs. Shelton looked in on her father-in-law, just to be sure he was all right. Mr. Shelton was not bedridden, but his activities were somewhat limited. He was 69 and had suffered for several years "from bronchitis, with complications." When Mrs. Shelton stopped by, he had come in from his walk and was sitting in a chair working out his selections for the football pool.

Whenever she found him at it and asked him how he planned to spend his winnings, he would say that he'd give most of them to George and her. "You two should have yourselves a real holiday," he would say. "Go to Blackpool or to Brighton. Take in the sea air. For myself? Oh, I'll keep back a few quid for myself and buy a better inhaler. I could use one, couldn't I, the next time I'm feeling chesty?"

Mrs. Shelton knew that her father-in-law had only a few more years to live. At one time the doctor had explained his condition to her, and the course it would most likely follow. The upper portion of his lungs—the bronchi, they were called—were already impaired severely. Maybe it had been the heavy cigarette smoking he'd done once, maybe not. Cigarettes, the doctor had said, plus damp air, plus cold, plus the rough lot he'd had as a child—put them all together, and over the years they led often enough to chronic bronchitis. At any rate, the impairment of the upper part of the lungs had placed an additional strain on his heart, and then the lower part of his lungs had become involved—meaning that besides bronchitis the old man also suffered from a touch of emphysema.

She remembered what the doctor had told her about the emphysema. How there were millions of little air sacs in a person's lungs—700 or 800 million tiny, invisible balloons—each with its own elastic walls, and how these walls would overstretch and then burst while trying to perform an extra share of the lungs' work. And this meant, as the emphysema grew worse, that a new strain was put on a person's heart.

Whether her father-in-law would eventually die of the emphysema, or the bronchitis, or just of a tired and worn-out heart, didn't of course make any difference. The idea now was to drop in on him once in awhile (just as some of his neighbors did) to make sure he was comfortable and to see if he needed or wanted anything special.

On Wednesday afternoon he was fine, though. It was such a lovely day in Stepney that it was hard for her to think about things like burst-out lungs and illness and dying. Mr. Shelton had brushed and combed his thinning hair. He was smiling. He was feeling perky and was extremely optimistic over his chances in the football pool. He said he had a very likely list of winners this time, he did.

Dr. Brian Williston was one of metropolitan London's more than two dozen Medical Officers of Health. His borough bordered on the Thames. From his office window he had a view, on a clear day like the present one, of row after row of chimney pots on the roofs of private homes, several smoking factory stacks, and the neighboring electrical generating plant—one of thirty-two scattered about the city.

Directly below the window, across an open courtyard, Dr. Williston could see a young man repairing a motorcar. His name was Amberson. He ran a small garage and lived above it with his pretty, red-haired wife. Amberson was often out-of-doors all day, tinkering with somebody's auto.

Dr. Williston knew the Ambersons well enough to nod and exchange a few words whenever he happened to meet them outside his office. He knew a good many of the people in his borough, at least casually. He had long made a point of meeting as many of them as he could, for he was interested in his borough charges as individuals, not merely as statistical elements in some dry and formal municipal report.

So often, though, an M.O.H. almost found himself forgetting that he *was* dealing with people and human needs, not just with words and numbers. The paperwork was endless. There were chest clinic reports to be made out, reports of the borough's X-ray services, reports of bacteriological examinations, not to mention those concerning old peoples' welfare, public health nuisance summonses, building drainage, smoke abatement and wind-born deposits, the public mortuary, and the Rodent Suppression Service—dear God, sometimes the list seemed to be absolutely infinite. But the *practice of medicine* and the *people* who lived in the borough whom you were really trying to serve and protect—well, at times, if you weren't careful, you almost forgot they even existed.

There were days when he felt that as a Medical Officer of Health he wasn't really a doctor at all but merely another municipal administrator, and there were plenty of *them* in every borough, and plenty more besides over at the County Council, drifting about the endlessly winding corridors of the County Hall.

Dr. Williston turned from the window and the city's blue evening sky and sat down at his desk. He was not a young man any more. He was over sixty, only two or three years from the mandatory retirement age. But he didn't *feel* old, not in the least. Damned if he'd retire because of some arbitrary bureaucratic ukase; he'd figure some way around it. They weren't going to pension him off and cast him onto the waste pile; he'd see to that.

The doctor turned the pages of his calendar pad. Thursday didn't look at all promising: a restaurant food-poisoning complaint to investigate further; a visit to one of the borough's hospitals and to some rooming houses to discuss old peoples' welfare procedures.

Friday might turn out better. A Roman Catholic nursing home, destroyed by bombs during the war, had recently been rebuilt. At 2:30 P.M. the new bishop was to dedicate the home; people said the bishop was an interesting man, and Dr. Williston had been wanting to meet him for quite some time. Other doctors from the borough would be there, too, and he'd have a chance to talk with them and hear about their patients. Even at secondhand, a little bit of medicine was better than none.

He circled the hour on his calendar pad. *Dedication of R.C. nursing home.* It sounded like an interesting appointment.

Wednesday, December 3, an almost perfect winter's day, drew to an end. At Kew Observatory, the weather had been fine and clear; winds had ranged between 8 and 13 knots out of the north; visibility had been excellent, never less than a mile and as much as 9 miles during the morning hours. To the east, at Kingsway, winds had been 10 to 14 knots, and visibility had varied from a mile-and-a-quarter to three-and-a-half miles. Temperatures in the city had been mild: a mean of 39 degrees.

Atmospheric deposits at County Hall had again increased a small but inconsequential amount: .61 milligrams of black matter, and .220 parts of sulfur dioxide had been recorded.

At the London Meteorological Office in Kingsway, the leisurely course of the high-pressure anticyclone had been charted carefully. The system's center still lay several hundred miles to the northwest. There was no way of telling when it would drift over the city or for how many hours afterward its effect would be felt.

The problem was routine and aroused little interest. The day just ending had been extraordinarily fine, which, in wintertime London, was much more remarkable. On such an agreeable evening it was difficult to shift one's point of view and to imagine that danger could be approaching—that an ordinary anticyclone might suddenly become motionless and remain so for more than a hundred hours.

Twenty

THE WEATHER in London began to deteriorate on Thursday, December 4. Morning temperatures were lower than on the previous day. The air was damper, the winds moderate and beginning to fall. Low banks of gray clouds frequently obscured the sky, and after the early hours there was very little sunlight.

At the Meteorological Office, a continuing watch was being kept on the progress of the anticyclone that now covered a considerable portion of Scotland, Ireland, and north-central England. The mass of cold air was following a predicted course, bringing with it conditions which normally produced periods of heavy fog. If these conditions persisted for more than a few hours, a thick pea-souper was very likely to develop that evening in the Thames valley.

The duration of the fog would, of course, depend on the forward progress of the anticyclone; this, in turn, would be affected by the strength of the low-pressure system propelling it from behind. Not until this second system had arrived could weather conditions hope to improve much in London; indeed, they could only grow worse.

If there was a danger signal, it was to be found to the west of Ireland, over the open Atlantic. The low-pressure system located there looked rather weak. Unless it deepened and picked up considerable strength, it might very well not be able to push on to the Thames valley for the next 48 hours, or perhaps even longer.

Most healthy Londoners gave little thought to Thursday's moist, chilly weather. They were inured to unpleasant December days. If a slight smell of smoke seemed to linger in the air and an unusual number of ash specks seemed to filter down through the gray overcast, they blamed these disagreeable effects on the nearest power station, especially the giants so prominently positioned along the river banks at Barking, Woolwich, Deptford, Battersea, and Fulham.

The smoky air certainly did not prevent Michael Watts from putting in a hard day's work at the football grounds or Angela Burke from walking along Marylebone High Street during her lunch hour to inspect the front of the hairdressing establishment she was going to visit on Saturday. And she *was* going there, no matter what her mother might say or "God in His wrath" might do to her afterward.

The leaden skies, the falling winds, the damp, close air certainly did not prevent Jerry Briggs from driving his car west to London Airport during the early hours of the afternoon, nor did they prevent Ethel's plane from arriving on schedule. She waved when she caught sight of him across the barrier at Customs, but when she and her friend were allowed to pass through, he could tell from her expression that something was wrong.

And there was. Ethel—it could only happen to her. She'd somehow managed to lose her suitcase. At least the airline people couldn't locate it yet. "Leave it to me," he told her. "I'll see if I can't get them to look a little harder."

He had the feeling that his smile wasn't as cordial as it might have been.

A few Londoners, though, were very much aware of the changing weather. Mary Chapman took her baby out for a long stroll in the morning, almost all around Little Stanmore, but after lunch the air seemed so chilly and raw and the sky looked so gray and threatening that she decided it would be better to keep Albert indoors.

Her mother said she would stay at home and watch the baby and urged her to go out and have some time to herself. The chance was too good to miss. She took the bus to Oxford Street and on the spur of the moment bought a new pipe for

John. A very handsome one, with a silver band around the stem. She hadn't meant to spend any money, but she was feeling so happy about the way Albert had improved the last few days that she let herself be carried away. She was sure John would understand when she explained; the pipe was really a gift from Albert. To celebrate his being well for almost the first time since they had brought him home from the hospital.

In the late morning, Dr. White walked slowly east, as far as Belgrave Square, but he did not venture out again in the afternoon. The air had not been particularly pleasant in the morning. His cough had returned—rather violently, once or twice. After the spasms and a moment or two of choking, he went to the bathroom and gave himself a small injection of adrenalin, the antispasmodic he generally administered to dilate the bronchi and ease the breathing passages. There had been a brief flurry with his heart just after his return from the Square. The fluttering had soon subsided.

He absorbed himself during the afternoon in the book about the Valley of the Kings. He'd never realized before that the tomb of Tutankhamen—the legendary "King Tut" —had been discovered by an expedition whose patron, Lord Carnarvon, had suffered from bronchitis. Illness had first brought the titled Englishman to Egypt. Otherwise he might never have visited the country, and the tomb might never had been excavated. How odd it was to think that there could be a connection between a pair of diseased lungs, the unhealthy winter climate in England, and the discovery of a royal Egyptian tomb.

Dr. White was not pleased by the late afternoon weather forecast. Friday would be cold. There would be light, variable winds and widespread fog at first in London, southeastern and eastern England. The fog might persist all day in places. A glance at the afternoon sky deepened his suspicions that a nasty 24 hours might lie ahead. The slight but persistent tightness in his chest seemed to confirm it.

In South Norwood, Mrs. Wilcox studied the dark sky with a sense of uneasiness. Because of the effect on her breathing, she often could tell beforehand when "something was coming." As early as Thursday morning she had an uneasy feeling that a cold, foggy spell might be on its way.

She feared the thought of really bad weather, as many bronchitics did, especially the elderly and those who lived alone. The hours of troubled sleep, and then the moment when you awoke in the dark with a burning sensation in your throat, and as you fought for air, sometimes coughing and gasping, you wondered dimly if you would ever be able to fully catch your breath and whether, solitary in the dark, you would still be alive at dawn.

If only Mr. Wilcox had been home—she stifled the thought. His ship was steaming westward, somewhere between Bombay and the Suez Canal.

A telephone call before lunch, though, changed everything. Amy, her niece, was in trouble. At their new flat. The flue in the fireplace was blocked, and the repairman wouldn't be able to have a look at it until Monday. Amy was afraid to keep her four-week-old baby much longer in a flat without heat. Was there room for them to stay over the weekend?

The invitation was quickly given. Mrs. Wilcox had plenty of room for Amy and the baby, and for Harold, too. They could stay as long as they liked. She started to put linen on the beds, the moment she'd hung up the phone.

By early evening Amy and her husband and the baby were all in the house at South Norwood. Mrs. Wilcox had everything ready for them, including a steaming hot dinner, and beer for Harold because he *was* somewhat partial to it. Having company cheered her immensely. She really had been craving some lately. She hadn't realized how much.

And she owed it all to the faulty flue in their new flat. It was inconvenient for them but nice for her. Otherwise, she would have been completely alone in the house during the entire weekend.

≈

After sundown, the light winds began to fail throughout Greater London. In the still air, the smell of smoke became more pronounced. Temperatures fell, and as the night grew colder, natural fog began to form along the winding course of the Thames. Soft, misty patches could be seen hanging low over the water, upstream, to the west, near the locks at Teddington, above the quays and bridges in the heart of the metropolis itself, and all along the shoreline, over the cranes and docks, the warehouses and storage terminals, eastward to Tilbury and Gravesend, guarding the mouth of the estuary. Fog at almost every turn and twist of the river—and imperceptibly growing denser.

≈

Still, the evening was pleasant enough, considering the time of year. Many London residents found it so, and in Hampstead, Jerry Briggs undoubtedly did. To his disbelief, Ethel was proving something less than a complete pill. He had managed to recover her suitcase at the airport, and though it really hadn't been a particularly difficult feat, she seemed to believe that it had, and all through dinner kept referring to it as though he'd gone out and climbed Mount Everest or something.

But after dinner, Ethel began to revert more to type. She said she wasn't the least bit tired, no, not the least bit, and since her friend wasn't either, what could he do but invite them for a spin around London to have their first look at the city, while Dotty cleaned up the kitchen and stayed with the kids?

He showed them the Strand and St. Paul's, Trafalgar Square and the Nelson Column, and drove them along Whitehall and then the Embankment for awhile, until the mist made him turn north to higher ground again. Ethel's friend—her name was Abigail Schwartz—"Call-me-Abby"—appeared to be a decent sort, even though, like Ethel, she never seemed to get tired or to know when she ought to have had enough. On the way home, she said the air smelled funny, kind of smoky, and he replied, "Well, that's London for you, Abby." Ethel said, "Jerry's been here six months. He's an expert." Typical of Ethel. Just typical.

He wasn't heartened much, either, when he heard the late weather on the BBC. *Fog*. Thick, persisting through the day in some sections.

Suppose it lasted into Saturday and they had to close down the airport? Suppose he was stuck with Ethel for an extra night?

Hour by hour the center of the anticyclone drifted closer to the city. As yet the huge mass of cold air gave no hint that it might lose forward motion and come to a complete halt. Its front edge, though, already had passed over the city, and this made it plain that for a time at least, poor weather conditions were apt to prevail in the Thames valley.

And so, during the evening hours of the fourth, appropriate agencies and services were alerted. The Metropolitan Police, the Port of London Authority, the Automobile Association, the Ambulance Service, all knew by late Thursday, either through their own facilities or through information furnished by the Meteorological Office, that considerable fog could be expected during the next twenty-four hours. It would probably linger and drift, and veteran weather-watchers began to wonder if the first real pea-souper of the season might not be about to descend.

Another working day was over now for many Londoners, and the city was beginning to shut down for the night. At Earl's Court preparations had been completed to receive the prize sheep, hogs, and cattle scheduled to arrive the following morning to be exhibited in the Smithfield Club's annual livestock show. Seventy-nine years before, during the prolonged and deadly smog of 1873-74, another famous livestock show had been held in London. Many valuable animals had been destroyed at the time, and amid a clamor of protest, the caustic observation had been made that sometimes in England it seemed as if less importance was attached to human life than to the lives of thoroughbred cattle.

Soon the doors at Earl's Court would be opened, and the animals would enter their stalls. Hogs and sheep on the second floor, cattle on the first. At Earl's Court, history, almost shamelessly, was at the point of repeating itself.

A number of London's citizens had dined well on Thursday evening, among them a group of hospital administrators and their wives who had enjoyed a convivial dinner in the West End. There had been several speeches, including the one just being concluded by a knowledgeable member-of-the-staff of the London Emergency Bed Service.

An independent charitable organization, the Emergency Bed Service worked through the city's four district hospital boards in cooperation with the Ministry of Health. The main function of the Service was to assist physicians in placing their patients in hospital; with more than two hundred general hospitals in London, and with their facilities frequently overtaxed, it was sometimes difficult for a general practitioner to know just where to send his patient for immediate care. When a doctor had experienced trouble placing a patient in one or two nearby hospitals, he called the E.B.S., and the Service, through its information room, often could facilitate matters and see to it that his patient was placed in hospital promptly.

The member-of-the-staff was completing his address, when, almost as an afterthought, he said to his listeners that he had a hunch—they had better remain on their toes during the next few days. Applications at the Service had been increasing for several weeks. Recalling the influenza epidemic of the previous year and other critical episodes of the past, he reminded them that December and January were notoriously bad months for all of them—a time when the demand was heaviest at the E.B.S.

"Watch out," he said, half seriously, half in jest. "When our applications are on the rise, as they are now, you never know what's in store."

He didn't mention smog, for he was not clairvoyant. Probably he was just thinking of another flu epidemic. Still, as some of the guests were to remark later, it really *was* an uncanny piece of timing no matter what he might actually have had in mind.

Thursday, December 4, was almost at an end. Visibility had declined sharply during the past six hours, from three-quarters of a mile to a quarter of a mile at Kingsway, from about a mile to a mere 88 yards at Kew. Temperatures were lower and in some localities already below freezing. To keep a bit of warmth in their homes, many Londoners heaped extra coal on their fires and then banked them. The fires would smoke heavily all through the night.

Atmospheric pollution apparently had been within a normal range for the entire day. Only .44 milligrams of smoke and .144 parts of sulfur dioxide had been recorded at County Hall. But these official measurements were misleading. They were based on a 24-hour period which had ended at 4:30 P.M., rather than at midnight. Until perhaps midday on Thursday, the air had been comparatively clean; after that, the city's atmosphere had become considerably contaminated. In all likelihood, at some undisclosed hour during the late afternoon or early evening, a temperature inversion had begun to form over many sections of Greater London, trapping the city's mixture of pollutants in the moist, stagnant air. By midnight, the fog already was being converted into smog.

In one quarter, conditions already were growing hazardous. Along the river, all the way from Gravesend to Teddington, a distance of 92 miles, the fog was not merely thick, it was impenetrable. At midnight, the Port of London Authority announced that all navigable sections of the Thames were fogbound. The great port shut down, river traffic ceased—

and the killer smog, drifting across the valley floor, little by little began to take the city into its grasp.

Twenty-one

DURING the early hours of Friday morning, the sleeping metropolis slowly began to stir again. Millions of new fires were lit, millions of electric appliances switched on; soon, additional tons of smoke, fly ash and sulfur dioxide were floating gently upward, unseen, into the cold, motionless air. The smog thickened and expanded. Gradually it spread, in an uneven pattern, over most of the 693 square miles of Greater London.

As daylight came, residents peered from their windows to discover that the weather predictions had been all too accurate. Fog was everywhere. Patchy in one location, dense in another, it seemed to shut out the sky and to give the wintry morning a look of bleak hostility. Perhaps it would clear off later in the day. All but the worst fogs generally did.

Londoners ate their breakfast of eggs and toast and gammon, swallowed an extra cup of tea or coffee to ward off the damp, and then, hunching themselves into winter jackets and coats, stepped out into the gray drifting smog. There was nothing to caution them that they might be entering a new and dangerous realm; as far as anyone knew, it was just another pea-souper or, if you had a more literary turn of mind, another London particular.

One of the first men who prepared to leave home on Friday morning, even while it was still dark, was James Allen. He lived about five miles south of London Airport, on the outskirts of Weybridge.

Mr. Allen worked for the London Transport Board.

He was a Green Line control inspector and was due at his garage in Staines, a low-lying suburb near the Thames, at 5:00 A.M.

Anticipating mud, he pulled on his gum boots, shut the back door of the house and picked up his bicycle. The fog looked thick. Exactly how thick, it was impossible to tell in the dark. But he'd set off in many a fog before, and he didn't intend to make any concessions to this one.

His usual shortcut saved him ten or fifteen minutes getting to the garage. It meant wheeling his bicycle across the back field until he came to a farmer's gate, then pedaling along a country lane till he reached the main road, finally following this directly into town. The other way round meant going out the front of his house and taking the main road directly; it came to an extra mile or so of travel.

Ordinarily, it took him about five minutes to cross the field. He pushed ahead slowly now, for the fog seemed extremely thick, worse then he'd believed at first. Visibility was only a yard or two. Things were as bad as he'd ever seen them.

Somewhere in the field ahead, perhaps fifty feet from the farmer's gate, there was a large tree. He was sure that in another minute or two it would begin to loom out of the misty darkness. He might even stumble into one of the lower branches if he didn't take care.

After awhile, though, he came to a halt. He couldn't see a single, blessed thing. He listened, but there wasn't the faintest sound. Mr. Allen looked at his watch. He'd been walking for a full ten minutes. Plenty of time to cross the field. Somehow, he'd missed the tree—and the gate as well.

He peered around again, but there was still nothing to be seen. He hadn't a clue as to how far he'd come or what part of the field he might be in. He decided to press forward, cautiously, to avoid stumbling into a hedge or a ditch. Sooner or later he was bound to make out the tree, or at least to meet up with a segment of the fence.

After walking another ten minutes, Mr. Allen had to admit the obvious. He was lost—in the same sixty-acre field behind his house that he'd crossed every working day for the past eight years. As far as he could tell, he might have been heading in any direction. He didn't have the slightest idea if he was facing north or south, toward the gate or away from it. He glanced at his watch a third time. It was 5:00 A.M. He was already due at the garage.

There really was no choice now but to push on again, wheeling the bicycle slowly until he came to something he recognized. The field was muddy, but at least his feet were still dry. The silence was complete, except for the squishing sound he made each time he drew one of his boots out of the mud.

Suddenly he rammed into something with the front of his bicycle. At first he thought that he'd finally reached the farmer's gate. A closer look told him he was mistaken. He had been walking in a circle for the past half hour and was standing by the house, right where he'd started. He had bumped into his own back fence.

Feeling a new sense of respect for the fog, Mr. Allen decided to play it safe this time. He went around to the front of the house, mounted his bicycle, and began to pedal along the road in the direction of Staines.

The going still wasn't easy, though. Things were growing a bit brighter as the night faded, but even so, he could only see ahead two or three yards. It was quite tricky, keeping to the road. He had to turn on his bicycle lamp to guide himself by the reflection it made in the string of "cat's-eyes" along the shoulder. He moved at a snail's pace, just turning the wheels enough to maintain balance.

The road was utterly deserted. For perhaps a mile he didn't pass a soul. The stillness was incredible. It was so complete that it made you wonder if some disaster mightn't have taken place and you were the last man left in the world.

Without warning, the silence was broken in the most awful way. The sound come from directly ahead—a half-cry, a half-groan. He braked to a stop and listened. It came again. An unearthly sound. Nearer this time.

He dismounted and stood in the road, both feet planted,

peering into the mist. There was a movement, and something began to emerge from the gray shadows. A flicker of white, and then a curious form seemed to rise up in the middle of the road. He saw the curving neck and the heavy body, clumsy now because it was out of its element. A ruddy swan, that's what it was. A ruddy swan from the river.

Mr. Allen drew back to the shoulder of the road and began to let the bird pass. They were all right to watch from a distance, but because of their bad temper, it didn't pay you to draw too close. As he watched the swan lumber by, a thought struck him. The Thames was at least a half mile away—what was the damn bird doing all the way up here?

Plainly, it was lost. As lost as he himself had been in the field a few minutes ago. The creature must have traveled away from the river a few yards and then hadn't been able to find its way back. Now it was wandering up the middle of the highway, trying to locate the water—and going in exactly the wrong direction.

Mr. Allen watched the swan pass by, and when it had disappeared into the fog again, he remounted his bicycle. A quarter of an hour later he was finally in Staines, approaching the garage.

The motor coaches were on the forecourt waiting to go out. The night-staff engineers had gotten them ready. Mr. Allen found a few of the drivers and conductors there ahead of him. They were men who lived near the garage. Some had biked in, some had walked.

The London Transport System, in common with the Metropolitan Police, the Postal and Ambulance Services, the Automobile Association, and the Port of London Authority, was staffed with men who had experienced heavy weather before. During wintertime they expected a certain amount of fog, and when it occurred they went about their work calmly, following whatever prescribed procedures their particular organization might have evolved. In the absence of specific instructions, they fell back on common sense. If conditions were especially bad, they used any expedient that seemed suitable—sometimes it was nothing more than the familiar wartime method of "muddling through."

Few of the motor coaches at Staines left on time Friday morning, but Mr. Allen got all of them off eventually. He sent them out with a good supply of flares—long staffs of wax and cord—which the conductors would light and carry ahead of the vehicles, if the fog proved too thick for the drivers to see unaided.

The Green Line coaches provided an express service for the huge suburban area surrounding the metropolis. Ordinarily the coaches ran from one of 30 main garages, like the one at Staines, through London and on to a number of other towns on the far side of the capital. A typical route was the one from Staines that followed the river eastward, all the way to Northfleet and Gravesend.

But on Friday morning an emergency plan began to go into effect. Many of the usual trips were curtailed. The coaches, instead of entering central London, approached only as far as the outskirts of the city. Then they turned around and headed back to their home garage. In this way, they continued to provide the suburban areas with a somewhat reduced service, without becoming snarled in the traffic jams that were bound to form in the more built-up sections of the metropolis.

After Mr. Allen had watched the last coach leave the forecourt, he sat down at his desk with a mug of tea and a biscuit. It was going to be a hard day for everyone, the drivers and conductors, the mechanics and supervisory personnel. But they had to keep the routes open if possible. All along the roads people would be standing in the wet, chilly fog, waiting for the coaches. Most of them would be trying to get to their jobs. A lot of the coaches would be late arriving. They would be even later getting back to Staines.

Mr. Allen thought of the swan wandering up the road. In all his years with London Transport he'd never seen anything like it. He told himself that this pea-souper was going to be a real ruddy mess before it got done.

Conditions in many parts of Greater London were not yet severe, although by late morning all riverside areas were heavily affected. Westminster and other districts near the water reported a thick, yellowish fog everywhere. Visibility was almost nil on the Thames itself and was less than a dozen yards around the Houses of Parliament. A few localities in central London were still relatively clear, and in some, pedestrians could catch the vague outline of buildings, as far distant as 70 or 80 yards.

But the smog was unquestionably growing thicker. As it did, familiar landmarks began to disappear. Shortly after noon, an observant passerby in Trafalgar Square noticed that the huge figure on top of the Nelson Column, 185 feet above the ground, was gradually receding into the mist.

The Underground was still maintaining a normal schedule, but the city's double-decker buses had begun to experience delays. Traffic in the West End sometimes moved briskly, sometimes only at a vexing crawl. In the snarls and tie-ups of the morning rush hour, cars, trucks, taxis, and buses, often with idling motors, poured out a blend of noxious vapors in the already polluted air.

All morning long the city's coal-burning railway engines added clouds of smoke to the thickening haze. There had been fog throughout the Midlands during the previous night, and now many trains from the north were overdue. Two that came in from Scotland several hours late were special trains of fifty cars each. They carried hogs, sheep, and cattle for the Smithfield Club's livestock show. By the time the animals had been quartered at Earl's Court, their handlers could see that some of the cattle were experiencing difficulty breathing.

During the morning, pedestrians said that they had known heavier fogs than the present one but could hardly recall one that seemed "dirtier" or more obnoxious. At times, the yellow haze had a remarkably pungent and penetrating smell. Some people described the odor as "smoky." Others said it was distinctly "sulfur-like." Most Londoners shrugged and continued on their way. They had more important things to do than to try to identify the particular scent of a December pea-souper.

At first Dr. White failed to notice the sulfurous smell as he left his Knightsbridge flat on the way to visit his sister. The morning mail had come and with it his reservations. A single glance at the tickets was enough to make his mind leap ahead to the train, the dock at Marseilles, and the sparkling blue waters of the Mediterranean Sea. Metaphorically, at least, by the time he left home, he was already coming down the gangplank in Egypt.

It was only after he had hailed a taxi in the Brompton Road that he began to realize how strong the odor was and to notice how singularly yellow and ugly the fog looked. Of course bronchitics like himself were often excessively apprehensive about the atmosphere they breathed, but all the same, today's cold air did seem unusually irritating to the nose and throat. He began to cough, though only lightly at first.

The smell, as he told his sister afterward, was remarkably sulfurous. No doubt it was caused by the low-grade coal being burned all over the city, both in people's homes and in the power stations. According to what one read in the newspapers, it was the stations like Battersea and Fulham that were the principal culprits. But Londoners themselves were to blame, too. Smoke, sulfur dioxide, and moisture-ladened air—what a perfect irritant for the mucous membranes.

Difficult or labored breathing. Dyspnea. That was the trouble with retired doctors. Whenever they had the chance, they began to analyze their own symptoms. Even in a London taxicab in the middle of a fog.

To distract himself from glimpses of the slow-moving traffic and the yellowish mist hanging overhead, Dr. White allowed his mind to turn back to a story one of his former colleagues had told him down in the borough, years before. The man's name was Rush and he had been unfortunate enough to take a flat without first making a full investigation.

Rush had been the Chief Administrative Officer in the borough. During the 1930's he had kept a home in the suburbs because his wife wanted "better air" for their children. By 1946, though, the children were safely off at school, and Rush, who had never been fond of commuting, decided to return to the city.

He and his wife took a flat in Pimlico, hard by the Thames. They had a balcony overlooking the water. It was a handsome, modern flat, and the balcony was the *pièce de rèsistance*, appealing particularly to Mrs. Rush, who greatly fancied the idea of eating their summer breakfasts there.

It hadn't worked out that way because the building not only overlooked the river, it also stood rather near Battersea Power Station. A little to the northeast of the station, which placed their new home squarely in the prevailing airflow.

It wasn't long before Rush and his wife realized they weren't going to eat many breakfasts on that balcony of theirs. Not unless they wanted to fish dirt out of the marmalade each morning or drink their coffee while being half-asphyxiated by the stench of the smoke and gases from across the river.

Actually, after the first day or two, they didn't even try. They simply closed the balcony off, sealed the French windows as tightly as possible, and did their best to keep the dirt and soot out of the rest of the flat. Even then, the sills inside were usually covered in the morning with a coating of grime.

They stayed in the flat a year, until their lease was up. Then they moved. But before they did, the French windows fell off—right out into the middle of the balcony.

At first they couldn't imagine *why* the windows had fallen off. They found that the metal hinges had been eaten through. The building was brand-new, and the Rushes had been the first tenants in the flat. Which meant that in less than twelve months the hinges had been completely corroded by the daily stream of sulfur dioxide pouring down from Battersea Station.

As a doctor, he had been interested in Rush's story. Human lung tissue was known to be tough and resilient, but could it be expected to endure that kind of treatment more successfully than copper or brass? Was it any wonder, with the kind of air they were forced to breathe, that half the people in London complained of feeling chesty?

Dr. White did not remain long at his sister's house. She noticed almost at once that he looked paler than usual and that his breathing sounded a little "labored," as she expressed it.

Of course she was right, although he didn't acknowledge it. The journey across town had taxed his resources more than he cared to admit. Still, it wasn't pleasant to hear the truth from somebody else. Nor to be told that he had been foolhardy to come, and that he should have remained at home till the fog had lifted.

The air seemed even worse, once he was outside again. He walked to the corner to find a taxi, but apparently there was a dearth of them in the neighborhood just then. He hesitated. Then he began to climb uphill toward the nearest thoroughfare. In a block or two he ought to find a taxi, and once inside, he could lean back and rest.

He was forced to walk six blocks, instead, stopping every block and then going on. The fog was growing denser and the air colder. Before finding a taxi he had to cough several times into his handkerchief. The mucoid material was thick and yellowish-gray. Raising it brought only a little relief. If anything, the spasms exacerbated the burning in his throat and the tightness of his lungs.

The taxi driver was helpful. He did his best to get through the foggy streets as rapidly as possible, but there were inevitable delays. As they were reaching his address in Knightsbridge, a spasm of coughing seized him again. The driver came round and gave him a hand as far as the front hall.

Dr. White paused on the staircase, before climbing to the second floor. He was still sitting there when one of his neighbors passed by on her way out. She asked him if he was all right. He thanked her and said that he was.

When he reached his flat, he administered ½ a cc of adrenalin in oil for the bronchial congestion and 2 cc's of Mercuhydrin for his heart. He was feeling utterly drained and shaky—more exhausted than he had ever been in his life. And he was still having moderate palpitations of the heart.

The phone began to ring. It was his sister. She just wanted to be sure that he had gotten back safely through the fog. Was he really all right? For some reason, he didn't quite sound like himself.

He described his return, the way things were outside, and the delays en route. He said he was better now. He was going to rest for awhile. Till the morning, perhaps, when he'd be back on his pins again.

Dr. White took off his shoes and placed them to one side, under the bed. He stretched out and drew a light woolen blanket over his legs and feet. Then he raised the pillows, put his head back, and closed his eyes. The cough had subsided. Soon his breathing would be normal again, and the sharp pain in his chest would pass away.

Dr. White's nephew came to the flat in Knightsbridge as early as he could. It was well after closing time at the office because the journey through the fog had taken longer than usual.

His mother had called him in the afternoon. She was concerned. Uncle Charles had not looked well during his visit. Later, over the phone, she thought that he had sounded a bit vague. As though he was wandering. And with his heart already so weak . . . would it be too much for him to look in on his uncle, just to be sure?

There was no answer when he rang the bell, and he had to hunt up the owner of the building so that he could get into the flat with her passkey. It was dark inside. He found the switch and walked across the living room. The door to the bedroom was ajar. It was dark there, too. "Uncle Charles?" he called out. "Are you having a nap?"

When there was still no reply, he pushed the door wider. He switched on another light. His uncle lay on top of the bed, a blanket over him. He seemed to be sleeping peacefully.

"Uncle Charles?"

Again there was no answer. Dr. White's nephew crossed to the bed and shook his uncle gently by the shoulder. It failed to rouse him. He raised his hand and touched his uncle's forehead. As he did, his eye fell on the envelope from Thomas Cook. The coldness of his uncle's forehead told him that he would have no use for his ticket to Egypt now. This year the old gentleman had stayed in London a few weeks too long.

Twenty-two

THERE WERE some people, though, who exercised prudence on the first day of the smog. In Little Stanmore, Mary Chapman took a look out of the window and decided to keep her baby indoors until the weather had improved. He remained quite comfortable all during the day. His breathing was fine, his color as healthy as she'd ever seen it. His appetite was exceptionally good. There was nothing on Friday to alter her faith in the virtues of a dry house.

Across the city, in Stepney, Mrs. Shelton stopped in for a moment or two after shopping to visit her father-in-law. He had not gone out, of course. He never did when there was fog. He told her that he was feeling "just a bit queer" with his breathing, and she saw that he was using his asthma inhaler from time to time. His bronchitis seemed no worse, though, than might have been expected, considering the weather outside. He was sitting up in bed, reading an account of the football matches that had been played earlier in the week. He said he didn't feel like eating, but when she told him she was going to have his favorite dish for dinner—fish and chips—he changed his mind. Mrs. Shelton said she would bring some over later and returned to her own home around the corner, assured that the old man was getting along as well as could be hoped.

On the south side of the river, Dr. Williston sat in his office at the borough's Health Department and checked his afternoon appointments. At two-thirty the bishop was to dedicate the rebuilt Roman Catholic nursing home. Dr. Williston put on his coat and hat and walked downstairs. It was just after 2:00 P.M. when he left the building.

Outside, he found the streets hazy with fog. There were misty halos around the street lamps, which had been turned on since noon. He had seen much denser fog in London, but the one today struck him as being singularly unpleasant. Perhaps it was the heavy smell of smoke that permeated the raw, clammy air.

On the way to the nursing home, he fell in step with Dr. Geoffrey Roberts, one of the younger men practicing in the borough. He knew Roberts quite well. Soon the G.P. was telling him about some of his recent cases.

He learned that a blind patient had been in Roberts' office the other day. The younger man described the visit, and for awhile they discussed the question of lost vision and the marshaling of the other senses as an act of compensation.

Then, while walking along, they began to talk of the fog. Dr. Williston said that today's pea-souper seemed rather "different" from the ordinary variety. For one thing, instead of being gray, it had a curious, yellowish-amber tinge. For another, although visibility was reasonably good, the quality of the air seemed worse than one would have expected. Somehow the fog appeared dirtier and more obnoxious than usual.

Dr. Roberts nodded. There might be something different about today's fog. He had first begun to wonder when he realized how busy he had been kept all during the morning. Mostly, he'd been seeing the end-stage bronchitics and asthmatics in his practice. Some of them had started to experience more acute trouble breathing. One or two were exhibiting the first symptoms of edema, and fluid, of course, in the absence of other causes, would indicate cardiac failure, associated with the later stages of bronchitis and emphysema.

Dr. Williston pointed out something more. Over the years, he had observed that edema and cardiac failure generally occurred only two or three full days *after* the arrival of a heavy fog. And yet some of Roberts' patients apparently were in serious trouble already—after only four or five hours.

The situation, they agreed, seemed rather curious. It was certainly the kind of thing that would bear watching.

Dr. Williston had a chance to talk with two or three other G.P.'s after the dedication ceremonies were over. All said that a number of their bronchitics were having a difficult time breathing. None of them could recall such a rapid response to the onset of fog.

Shortly after three o'clock, Dr. Williston began to walk back to his office. Perhaps his imagination was starting to play tricks, but during the hour or so that he'd been inside the nursing home, the fog seemed to have grown considerably thicker. The smell was more noticeable, too. He began to cough and had to clear his throat several times before he finally reached the front of the building.

Dr. Williston sat at his desk for a minute or two and tried to collect his thoughts. The health of the borough was his responsibility. Ordinarily, he was not a man given to vague worries or hasty fears, but now—he had to confess —he was gravely concerned. Something clearly was wrong out there in the streets. After a mere four or five hours, the fog was greatly hampering the breathing of chronic chest cases. The speed of the thing was absolutely without precedent. Perhaps what disturbed him even more was the fact that the doctors he'd talked with served patients in widely scattered areas. Apparently the entire borough was being affected.

The doctor looked down at his desk. At first, he was too amazed to credit what he saw.

He hadn't noticed before, but now he realized that his hands were absolutely filthy. Completely black. "My God," he thought, "what's happened to me?"

He rubbed his thumb and forefinger together. They were covered with soot.

When he arose and went to the washroom, he saw that his face was smudged and that his collar was filthy, too. A bitter taste seemed to linger in his mouth. Suddenly the cough returned, deep and hacking. When the spasm was over, his throat felt painful and raw, from one side to the other.

Dr. Williston washed his hands and face and tried to remove some of the soot from his shirt collar. Afterward, instead of returning to his office, he walked slowly upstairs to the roof.

Once there, he went over to the edge and looked around. Despite the pervasiveness of the amber haze, it still was possible to see forty or fifty yards in every direction. To the north, toward the Thames, there was a manufacturing plant with a single, tall chimney. The top of the chimney, at a height of 150 feet, was barely visible.

Dr. Williston looked at it—and received a second shock. The smoke was not rising, as smoke normally did. Instead, it was curling around the top of the chimney and then coming down—*flowing* down, black clouds of it, straight toward the ground.

"My God," he thought, "it's an inversion. Like the Meuse valley. Like Donora. . . ."

As he returned to the stairs, he began to think of how the people in the borough might be alerted to the possible danger. Or better still, how the entire city might be alerted. For surely if his suspicions were justified, conditions in the borough were being duplicated in other parts of London.

He had read an account of the Donora disaster only a few months before. The people in Donora had assumed they were dealing with an ordinary fog of the sort that regularly occurred in their town. As a result they had wandered blithely about for two days and nights without taking even the most elementary precautions. They had failed to remain indoors whenever they could; they had not kept their houses shut up tight; they had worn no masks or handkerchiefs outside; worst of all, the chest and cardiac patients had never been warned to avoid unnecessary exertion.

For several minutes Dr. Williston considered what he might do. There was no plan for such a contingency. The city as a whole had none; the individual boroughs had none; the Ministry of Health had none.

He continued to be haunted by what he had heard from Dr. Roberts and the other men in the borough earlier in the afternoon. He remembered that in the Meuse valley and Donora smogs, serious illness—and death—had only begun to occur on the third day. Yet here in London, Roberts and the others had seen patients who were sick already, on the very first day of fog. Surely the implications were clear. What now was happening in the borough posed a substantial threat to people's health. The city's air was probably highly contaminated, and there was no telling how much worse it would get or how long the fog would last.

On the other hand, it would be difficult to prove just how poisonous the atmosphere in the city might already have become. Most of the usual measurements would be useless; they were made either once a week or once a month. The most significant readings were taken in the laboratory in County Hall. They were made daily, Tuesday through

Saturday, and then on Monday, for the weekend just past. But air pollution could shoot up to high levels in an hour or two. New readings should be made at County Hall immediately and continue to be made on an hourly basis while the fog lasted. He wondered how much support he would get for such a radical procedure from the authorities at County Hall.

Dr. Williston picked up his office phone and called the Medical Department at the London County Council to discuss what he had heard and seen that afternoon. The reception he received was not enthusiastic.

The authorities at County Hall appreciated the fact that a thermal inversion was a possibility. They considered it a remote one, however, their position being based on the then current theory that a thermal inversion was an extremely rare phenomenon. They acknowledged that the smoke from the factory chimney which Dr. Williston had seen descending to the ground was certainly suggestive but —of itself, and in the absence of more definitive evidence or criteria—it was hardly more than that.

After a lengthy conversation, Dr. Williston was informed that County Hall believed there was no inversion. London, he was told, was not in danger of experiencing a disaster or of becoming another Donora, Pennsylvania.

Naturally, the M.O.H. might take any steps that he deemed advisable in his own borough, but just as obviously, he could hardly hope to receive any encouragement from County Hall, where opposite views were held. And since his "proof" was, to say the least, rather flimsy, he might be well advised not to raise any unnecessary local alarms. No one, of course, would do anything to curb or suppress his opinions, but since County Hall did not agree with his suspicions, it could hardly be expected to do anything to translate them into action.

Dr. Williston stayed in his office until closing time. His mind was filled with fresh doubts. The men at the Council were *not* fools. They were sound medical people, and their opinions were supported by equally sound scientific technicians. The rarity of thermal inversions was a widely accepted

fact. And it was strange that no one else, not a single one of
his fellow borough M.O.H.'s, had made observations similar
to his own and called the Council, as he had done. Maybe
the smoking chim͟ ͟took had merely been a local phenomenon, a temp͟ ͟ ͟nfined to a
small area in his o͟ *took out the window to her indoors* ͟ *Ch 22*

The men at C͟
given to their vie͟
hasty conclusion͟
disperse before v͟
soon become ac͟

He stood at͟
sky. Across th͟
burrowing und͟
man had been͟
And there wo͟
corner of Lon͟

The doct͟ t
managed to g͟ it
County Hall 't
believe they could be.

Twenty-three

FOR MRS. WILCOX the early part of the day had passed
quite agreeably in South Norwood. She had eaten breakfast
with her niece and then had watched the baby being bathed
and dressed and fed. After lunch she said how nice it was to
have company this way, and Amy replied that it was even
nicer for Harold and herself to be there and to have a warm
place to keep the baby while they were waiting to move into
their new flat.

Despite the fog, Mrs. Wilcox decided to go shopping
during the afternoon. The unexpected arrival of her niece

and family meant that extra milk and some other food items would be needed over the weekend. Ignoring the damp weather, Mrs. Wilcox set off for the store.

Usually she didn't stay out too long when it was cold and foggy. But she had never made it a firm principle to remain indoors altogether. Dr. Speyer had told her once not to stay out in bad weather any longer than necessary. He also had said that she herself was the best judge of what was "too long." And when everything was said and done, as she'd explained to the doctor, she wasn't an invalid yet and didn't intend to make herself one either.

Coming around a foggy corner, she very nearly ran into a friend of hers named Maude Coffey. They exchanged a remark or two about the weather and then continued on together to the High Street, where they bought their groceries. When Maude said she was going on to the chemist to pick up a box of corn plasters, Mrs. Wilcox agreed to keep her company.

It was only two short blocks to the chemist, but Mrs. Wilcox didn't reach there. A few steps from the grocery she began to feel "queerish." A tightness in the chest and a strange dizziness in the head. "Maudie," she said, "I'm feeling the fog. I'll be going home now."

Her friend knew she suffered from bronchitis and so turned back with her, but Mrs. Wilcox had no trouble getting to the house. Before putting away the groceries, though, she did have to lie down on the sofa and rest for a few minutes. The dizziness quickly passed. Her breathing grew easier. She coughed a little, but after taking her medicine, the irritation stopped.

She cooked supper that night, even though she was still feeling a bit tired. When Amy volunteered to help with the dishes, she said that she could. She went to bed early, after the dishes had been put away. "I'll be better tomorrow," Mrs. Wilcox told herself. Soon, she felt her eyes growing heavy. She had no trouble falling asleep on Friday night.

Michael Watts gave little thought at first to the foggy weather. For a football groundsman like himself, poor visibility simply meant it would be that much harder to do a good day's work. In the morning, getting to the job took longer than usual. Buses in the East End were running behind schedule. Most of the other men came in late, too, although he was told that the Underground seemed to be operating without difficulty. Actually, much of the delay came after you'd left your Underground or bus stop and began to walk. In the street the fog was thick enough so that you had to keep a sharp lookout, or you might run into something.

Watts spent the morning and afternoon out-of-doors. He was responsible for the usual lawn maintenance and for the marking of the fields. He was also in charge of the pavilion dressing rooms. He spent little time there on Friday, though, except to have a bite of lunch out of the cold and damp.

Luckily, he had set up the guidelines the previous afternoon, so that when it came time to mark the field for Saturday's match, the limited visibility made hardly any difference. He was able to keep working at a fairly smart pace. Busy and absorbed, he scarcely noticed that the fog was growing thicker during the late afternoon. Toward quitting time he was surprised to find how dense it had become.

By then word had gotten around about the buses. They weren't running anymore. At any rate, not the ones that went by the football pitches. Maybe down at the Town Hall he might have some luck. Traffic was always heavy there. Usually there were lots of buses, and most times you had no trouble getting a seat for yourself.

It was three-quarters of a mile to the Town Hall. Not much of a walk for anyone in good shape. Watts put on his jacket and cap and set out from the pavilion.

After a block or two, he knew that he had never been in a fog like this before. It wasn't just the thickness of it. Today's fog was the wrong color. Not the ordinary gray kind of a fog at all. Actually, it looked black and "gauzy," much like the veils you saw women wearing at funerals. And it *was* dirty. Scummy and dirty, so that you could almost feel it drifting around you, hanging on to you like a sort of cold, clammy sheet.

The familiar streets had all but disappeared by now. At most he could see only a few feet ahead. Crowds of people were groping their way through the darkness. Sometimes they would stumble into each other. He saw one woman trip over the curb and nearly fall.

He began to cough long before he had reached the Town Hall. At first he didn't think too much about it, because he was too busy trying to make out where he was. He didn't actually know. Somehow he had taken the wrong turn and lost his way, even though he'd been all around the neighborhood a hundred times. After awhile he had to stop and ask a passerby for directions. No, he had to ask several people before he found someone who wasn't lost, too.

On an ordinary day, it would only have taken him fifteen minutes to reach the Town Hall steps. This time it took him more than an hour and a half. And it didn't do him much good when he got there. No buses were running by the Town Hall, either. And the Underground was no help. The line didn't come at all close to the street where he lived.

He'd have to walk the rest of the way home. It meant another half mile or a little more. The fog was even worse now, and at some of the main corners, the police had set out emergency flares. He began to trudge on again, very slowly. He coughed—much harder this time. What he brought up out of his chest was filthy. Thick and filthy. And the taste was disgusting.

Groping along, he began to wonder if there really was any end to the fog. The awful, trailing mist was everywhere. All around him. He felt as if he were wrapped up inside a tight, black, suffocating blanket, and there wasn't any way of getting out of it.

He coughed and spit into his handkerchief and fought for air. It was like being in the water and drowning. His nose and throat stung. His chest hurt. He wondered if he would get out of the black fog alive. A voice seemed to tell him to start running. In any direction—it didn't matter where—just to escape the fog.

For several minutes, Michael Watts struggled against panic. He felt icy cold. His shirt was wet through and stuck to his back. He didn't hurry, though. He kept his stride short and even, deliberately pacing himself like a long-distance runner. And every so often he stopped to have another look around, to cough, and to draw in a breath.

He very nearly felt like crying when he saw the store on the corner. It told him where he was. On his own block, less than a hundred feet from the house where he lived.

A few more steps, a turn, and he was inside the hallway. It was warm there. It was clean. A naked light bulb was shining brightly. It looked beautiful. And thank God, at last there was a little fresh air to breathe. Then he doubled over and coughed into his handkerchief. The stuff that came up was absolutely black.

At seven-thirty that morning, Michael Watts had left his small room in the East End, a robust man in perfect health. Although he didn't yet realize it, he had returned home twelve hours later with damaged lungs and health permanently impaired—a chronic bronchitic. The groundsman had been outside in the great killer smog for a single day.

Twenty-four

IN THE BEGINNING, Jerry Briggs had not been very impressed by the fog. There were only patches of it to be seen in Hampstead at breakfast time, and later, when he drove to work in Fleet Street, he wondered if the local residents would call the low overcast and the occasional swirls of gray mist a "real" pea-souper.

By late morning, the sky seemed to have grown darker.

Somebody switched on the office lights before noon, and he noticed, when he went out for lunch, that most of the other buildings in the neighborhood also were burning their lights.

During the afternoon Jerry Briggs paid hardly any attention to the weather. He was too busy working on a variety of stories. There was Sir Gerald Templer's latest press conference concerning the Malayan guerrillas, and there was the new and touchy Anglo-Iranian oil question. Then too there was the disappointing murder trial in Staffordshire, about which, unhappily, the insiders had been right, for nothing very lurid or spicy had emerged thus far to entertain an American audience. As far as Jerry Briggs was concerned, British crime was currently as unworthy of its great reputation as the vaunted British fog.

Things *were* a bit thicker that evening on the way back to Hampstead. Darkness had come, which of course didn't make driving any easier, but there were a number of flares lit at some of the busy intersections, and conditions might have been worse.

Oxford Street looked very strange. Traffic was frequently stalled, so that he had plenty of time to notice the Christmas trees decorating the store facades. The colored lights seemed to be hanging suspended in midair, surrounded completely by heavy, yellowish mist.

After turning north at Marble Arch, he found the fog even thicker for awhile. Fortunately, someone at the office had given him some tips for getting about, so he opened the windshield of his old, secondhand British-make car and at least kept the glass from clouding up inside. Lights on, of course. There was a string of about four or five buses ahead, and he simply tagged along after them, moving slowly, without any hope of passing. Eventually the fog grew thinner, and he succeeded in getting back to the apartment in Hampstead without further delay.

He still had some driving to do that evening. An English colleague and his wife had heard about the arrival of Dot's sister and very kindly had invited them all over for a party at their home, in a place called Holder's Hill, outside of

Hendon. The baby-sitter arrived just after seven, a high school girl who lived in the next block. At seven-thirty Jerry Briggs got behind the wheel again.

The drive north to Holder's Hill went off easily enough. There was considerable fog, but not nearly as much as there had been earlier in the center of town. The odd thing was how unevenly it seemed to be distributed. At some places, mostly where the roads dipped, you could scarcely see five feet ahead of the car; at other times, particularly after a few seconds' climb, you'd come up into a cold, starlit night with so much visibility all around that you could hardly believe there was any fog within a hundred miles.

Once they got to the party, Jerry Briggs quickly forgot about the fog. Something was wrong, but he didn't know exactly what. It was the way he felt—almost a little queasy. Halfway through his second highball he put down the glass. Maybe what he needed was to get some food in his stomach before he did any serious drinking.

They had a casserole and a salad, and then dessert and coffee. None of it tasted right to him. A brandy didn't help, either. The room felt stuffy, and things weren't improved a great deal when a couple of the other men lit up cigars. Someone said they shouldn't be smoking cigars—the air was bad enough already because the fog had started to get into the house. But they went on smoking anyway, and the air in the room kept on getting closer.

He really *didn't* feel at all like himself. When someone said that if the fog grew any worse the airports would have to shut down and when Dot pointed out that Ethel and Abby might have to stay over and book a later flight, it didn't seem to affect him one way or the other. Let Ethel and her chum do whatever they wanted. All that *he* wanted was to go back to the apartment and crawl into bed.

The party broke up early because the fog had gotten heavier and some of the people there were afraid they would have trouble getting home. Most of the guests were English, and they knew from experience what they were talking about.

He was surprised to find how bad things had become outside. The fog was gray and dense and covered the roads completely. It seemed to smell more, too, and when you swallowed some of it—and you could hardly keep from doing that—the stuff made you choke and cough and turn sick to your stomach.

The visibility was much poorer than on the way out. Sometimes he found that he could see a few yards, sometimes only a few feet. He opened the windshield again and drove very slowly, but even then he had a lot of trouble following the road. Finally, he asked Dot to open the door and look out on her side. By watching the shoulder, she could guide him left and right and tell him where he was.

When they got as far as Hampstead Heath, things seemed to clear for a minute or two. Then the fog returned. Their headlights picked it up coming toward them. Waves of it. Literally waves of fog—turned a sickly green color in the lights of the car.

Suddenly he put on the brakes and opened the door. Sweat was pouring off his forehead and temples. He tried to get out quickly, away from the car, but he didn't move fast enough. Bending over, he vomited in the middle of the road, gagged helplessly, and vomited again.

Then—God knows how much later—the nausea subsided a little. Dot asked him if he was all right to drive, and he said yes, sure. She continued to "steer" for him, though, keeping her door open and looking out to locate the whereabouts of the road. Somehow he got the car back and parked in front of their apartment again.

Inside, he felt better almost at once. The air was cleaner for one thing. Hardly any of the fog had gotten in. After awhile the nausea left him entirely, and he found that he was hungry. So they made him some tea and sandwiches and he wolfed them down. He said he felt like a damn fool getting sick that way.

Before midnight he had pulled off his clothes and was lying in bed. He stretched out heavily and was half asleep by the time his head touched the pillow. Whatever else was true, he had changed his mind about one thing. When the English put together a fog, they did a pretty damn good job of it.

The smog grew thicker all over London on Friday night. Areas previously spared now became heavily affected. In the oldest parts of the city, trailing clouds of dirty haze shrouded the Royal Exchange, St. Paul's Cathedral, and the Bank of England.

At neighboring Guildhall, badly damaged by fire during the war and still not fully repaired, the high commissioners of the Commonwealth countries were holding a reception for a thousand elegant and important guests. Smog drifted into the building and hung over the heads of cabinet ministers, diplomats, and members of the City Corporation. As the hour grew late, gentlemen in evening dress and ladies in velvet gowns and brightly colored saris could be seen groping their way outside to limousines and taxicabs. The first full day of the killer smog was over, and like the majority of people in the metropolis, the eminent guests leaving Guildhall complained about the foggy, miserable weather, without the slightest suspicion of the lethal properties in the air surrounding them, or any notion of what was actually taking place in the ancient capital.

By Friday evening, the toll of illness and death already was mounting rapidly in London. District nurses had treated more than twice as many respiratory cases as they had on the previous day; ambulance calls had increased by a third; deaths in the city had soared by over 50 percent.

The meteorological outlook had become far more menacing. During the late afternoon, the huge anticyclone had lost all forward motion; now, it was stalled over a wide area of southeastern England, the Channel, and northwestern Europe—its center located directly above the Thames valley and London itself. As a result there was a total lack of air movement in the city. A dead calm prevailed at Kew, Kingsway, and in every other quarter of the capital. No wind—which meant no dispersal of the vast amounts of pollution that were accumulating. And to make the situation worse, there was no way of knowing when the mass of still, cold air would move forward again, so that the atmosphere could begin to clear and the danger to pass.

No warning bulletins, however, were issued by the Meteorological Office, and no efforts were made by responsible officials to ascertain the current death rate or the amount of pollution in the air. Their belief remained fixed that an occasional pea-souper was quite inevitable, and that when it occurred, a few of the old and sick were bound to die. No wider calamity was anticipated or deemed possible by health authorities, weather experts, government personnel, or members of the press.

And so, at last, Friday, the fifth of December, came to its incredible end. For more than 24 hours, the great city of London had been experiencing a growing air pollution disaster, yet the astonishing fact was that hardly a soul in the city realized it or even suspected that there was the slightest danger.

Twenty-five

AFTER AN EXTREMELY cold and windless night, people in London awoke on Saturday, December 6, to find themselves engulfed by a smog that extended at least 20 miles in every direction from the center of the city. Visibility was even poorer than on the previous morning. At Kingsway it was less than 50 yards; at Kew it was absolute zero.

Every form of transportation was affected. During the night, London's main airport at Heathrow and the secondary airports at Northolt and Bovington had suspended operations; arrivals were being diverted to fields beyond the area of the smog, and all departures had been canceled.

Shipping on the Thames remained at a standstill. Long-distance trains from the west were arriving two hours late; some suburban lines were reducing service, and local trains were reaching the city as much as two and a half hours behind schedule.

By eight in the morning, most buses and Green Line express coaches were experiencing delays. A number of routes were without service, and nine garages were completely shut down.

Optimistic owners of private cars, heedless of icy roads and the blanket of smog, headed for central London; arriving there, they found conditions far worse than they had anticipated. More cautious owners left their cars in the garage and sought an alternate means of reaching town; as they did, the Underground received larger crowds than usual, and the trains began to run behind schedule for the first time.

As bad as things were on Saturday morning, the city could still claim that its transportation system was in partial operation. Breakdown and chaos, however, were only a short step away.

For many Londoners, the dense yellow fog drifting outside their windows on Saturday meant a sensible change of plans and the postponement of needless outdoor activities. Angela Burke decided that it was not a suitable day to have her hair done. For one thing, the fog was really so thick and dirty that no one would willingly go out in it unless they were forced to. So she would need to make up an excuse to explain why she was leaving the house, and it would all be a dreadful bother.

And for another thing, her mother was beginning to feel a bit chesty, as she always did whenever the weather turned bad. She was starting to complain and would soon take herself off to bed. And, of course, after that it would be "Angie, do this," and "Angie, do that," and all the housework would fall on *her* shoulders, so she'd have no time to slip out. It wasn't a great shame, really. The first thing next week—that's when she'd go.

On Saturday morning, Mary Chapman first began to think that perhaps there was something wrong with the baby. It was his breathing. Just a little difficulty that nobody else might have noticed. And not anything like the trouble he'd had in Hammersmith earlier in the fall.

She kept him indoors, just as she had done on Friday, and tried to keep the fog from getting into the house, too. Albert really did *look* fine, and even John said that he didn't think much was wrong.

Well, maybe she *was* imagining it because of the dark, foggy day. She would just have to wait and see how he was tomorrow. Perhaps the fog would lift, and with the Little Stanmore house snug and dry, he would be completely all right.

On Saturday, Mary Chapman worried—and waited to see.

In Stepney, Mrs. Shelton spent most of the day with her father-in-law, sharing the vigil with her husband, who was off from work during the afternoon. The old gentleman was clearly being affected by the fog. His breathing was heavy, and he had to use his inhaler even more than on Friday. He was in good spirits, though, and seemed to be almost his usual self. When she brought him the newspapers he was glad to have them. He read them as he always did, all the way through.

His appetite was very poor, however. He didn't complain of anything, no pain or discomfort, he just said he wasn't hungry. The only thing he had during the morning was a cup of Bovril. And then later on she gave him some milk, which he managed to swallow.

Mrs. Shelton didn't say anything to her husband, but she was concerned about her father-in-law. The fog was so thick, it couldn't be doing him any good. And it was very cold, too. Still, there was no help for the weather. If you lived in London it was just something you had to accept—knowing that most of the winter conditions would be quite bad a great deal of the time.

She believed that a London fog was as much a part of nature as the sunlight or the rain. The word "smog" meant nothing whatever to Mrs. Shelton.

Hardly anything worked out on Saturday as Jerry Briggs had imagined it would earlier in the week. He was late getting to breakfast, where Dotty informed him, as she reheated the coffee, that Ethel was staying on with them for awhile longer. The two girls didn't have any choice in the matter. London Airport had been shut down completely at eight-thirty the night before and their flight canceled. There was no telling when they might be booked on another.

It was funny, but he found that he didn't mind too much. "Trapped with Ethel in a London fog"—the idea was pretty hilarious, if you thought about it.

And she did come through on Saturday; afterward he had to admit it. She and her chum really managed to do all right in a pinch. The four of them were stuck inside the apartment with the kids with nowhere to go, and it might have been a mess if somebody hadn't thought of different ways to make the time pass.

That's when Ethel and Abby rolled up their sleeves and did a nice job. They made a game out of the fog, and they got the kids to play along. It became a sort of Swiss Family Robinson, with everyone lending a hand and taking turns doing chores, and that kind of thing.

Late in the morning everyone got dressed up to go on the expedition-for-supplies. It was Abby's idea, with strong support from Ethel. He didn't care much himself for taking the kids out into the fog, not even just to go as far as the grocery store, but everyone else jumped on him so hard that finally he had to say okay, okay.

So they set off, he and Ethel holding Kip by the hand, and Dot and Abby bringing along Gail, and the party sticking very close together because once you got outside and up the steps to the street, the fog was so thick you could hardly see in front of your nose.

The expedition was a big success. They got the supplies at the grocer's two blocks away and then succeeded in bringing everything safely home, with no members of the party lost or left behind and with no harm done except for Kip and Abby coughing a little and Dot and himself—in fact all of them—complaining about the way the fog made your eyes sting, as if there was some kind of acid in it.

Later, while the kids were taking their nap after lunch, it turned out that Ethel and Abby not only knew how to play bridge, they really weren't half bad at it. It was a great stroke of luck. Four people stuck with each other during a London pea-souper, and all four pretty fair bridge players.

He didn't come out and tell her so, but he did hint to Dot later on that her sister wasn't a bad sort, after all. He was forced to say so—the two girls were pretty good sports when you thought about it.

Dot agreed. She pointed out that Ethel and Abby were spending their vacation in a basement apartment in fog-bound London, instead of Switzerland as they'd planned. Good sports, Jerry Briggs had to admit it. And thank God for the Swiss Family Robinson.

Mrs. Wilcox was sick all of Saturday. She was beginning to have so much trouble breathing that she didn't even try to make the beds or to do the rest of her housework. She stayed in her room, where the coal fire was lit and things were a little warmer. The air inside was poor, though. There was no way to keep the fog out. Each time someone opened the front or the back door, it came into the house; it came in through the spaces around the windows, and even down the chimney. The house in South Norwood was pleasant, but it just wasn't very snug or tight.

Gray streaks of fog hung in her bedroom and almost hid the ceiling. The fog made her cough, and she had to keep taking her medicine every so often. Luckily, Amy was there to cook and to look after things. She couldn't have gotten on at all without her.

Another letter came from Mr. Wilcox during the morning, but she scarcely glanced at it. She didn't seem to care a great deal what it said. She took only a cup of tea for her lunch. Her breathing was noticeably heavier, and the pains in her chest were growing worse. Her head had begun to ache a little, too.

Amy said that if she didn't feel better soon, it might be a sensible idea to call the doctor. Her niece had worked as a trained nurse before she had married Harold. Now she was beginning to act like one.

Mrs. Wilcox said that a good rest was all that she needed. And to have the fire kept on, so the room would stay warm. Harold banked it for her, and she stretched out on her bed. Her chest and head weren't any better, though. Actually—and she didn't tell Amy—they seemed to be getting worse. But once the fog had lifted, she would soon be her old self again . . . another few hours, and maybe the weather would improve.

Twenty-six

FROM BEGINNING to end, Saturday was a nightmare for anyone in London who had to be out-of-doors. All the city's streets were filled with the thick, choking mist, and many soon became completely impassable. During the afternoon, instead of thinning, the smog seemed to become even denser.

Numerous buses were forced to halt in their paths and await the arrival of flares, before attempting to resume their journey back to their home garage. At one time, a procession of seventeen clumsy double-deckers, nose-to-tail, like a huge, red, metallic caterpillar, could be seen trying to poke along through the smog. The drivers took turns steering the lead bus, while the conductors, armed with spluttering flares, ran around in front and shouted directions.

At its headquarters in Leicester Square, the Automobile Association found itself inundated by appeals for information and assistance. The A.A. had almost three-quarters of a million members, and in the Operations Room at Fanum House, there were times when it seemed as if all of them were trying to reach the Whitehall exchange simultaneously. The thirty-odd operators there answered the calls as best they could; sometimes, no one in the room had a chance to put down his phone receiver for an hour at a stretch.

Many of the calls—primarily the early ones—were of the kind that Operations had to deal with on any routine day. Drivers were in trouble on the road; some lacked the necessary spare parts to make repairs themselves; others required a breakdown van to tow them off to a garage. And there were the usual inquiries about the best route available in crossing London for someone going to Kent or Surrey, or just a question or two about what the weather was like—better or worse than the latest bulletin on the BBC?

But as the hours passed, the inquiries began to change. More and more motorists called Fanum House to say that conditions were now too bad to continue driving. There was scarcely any visibility, not even with the aid of the many flares placed along the main thoroughfares and with all of the city's thousands of street lamps turned on. They were going to have to leave their cars somewhere until the fog lifted—what advice could the Association give them in the meantime?

The A.A. replied that a driver should leave his car in a "safe" place, provided that he could find one. The best spot would be on a side street, preferably near a lamppost. Motorists also were urged to leave their lights on to avoid having their cars struck by passing vehicles. The early assumption at Fanum House was that the fog would disappear in a few hours more; when it failed to do so, hundreds of batteries ran down in cars abandoned all across London.

By late Saturday afternoon, the Association's breakdown patrols and garage tow trucks were finding it increasingly difficult to reach stranded motorists. And for the first time in its history, the Association began to discourage members who wanted to drive to the capital.

"Is your journey really necessary?" Operations asked. "You can't get into London. And if you should somehow manage it, you won't be able to get out again."

Over and over, the weary operators in Leicester Square repeated their warnings. After a few hours, the calls grew fewer. The men and women in the Operations Room—like many other workers in the city—had long since given up any thought of returning home. There wouldn't have been any point to it; everyone knew by now that the fog wasn't going to lift, and the next morning they'd only have had to struggle back to the job again through smogbound streets. That night they slept on cots at headquarters, and most of them would do so again for two nights more.

The killer smog made extraordinary demands on the Metropolitan Police. Understaffed by more than 20 percent, the force of 14,600 officers and men worked around the clock to keep Greater London from slipping into wider confusion or panic.

The efforts of the police were strenuous and varied. Incredible traffic jams developed, and the bobbies from the local precinct stations had to disentangle them. Donning white "fog coats," some of them manned positions at major intersections, lit flares to guide motorists along the darkened streets, and abandoning their radio-equipped Humbers, organized makeshift traffic patrols on bicycle and foot.

Bizarre incidents took place, and often policemen were the ones to discover them. Typical was the motorist who set out from a hotel in Mayfair to drive to nearby Battersea. An officer found him sitting in his car in the middle of a cemetery. The driver couldn't explain how he'd arrived
there, especially without knocking down a few of the tombstones. The officer couldn't explain it, either.

All over the city motorists had completely lost their

bearings. One police patrol car, still managing to operate south of the river, came upon a line of vehicles apparently stalled. Leaving his own driver in the Humber, the sergeant groped his way forward to the first car. The lady inside was trying to reach her home in Croydon; she hadn't the faintest notion where she was.

The sergeant walked back along the line of cars, asking, "Who wants Croydon?" Finally a convoy of eight vehicles was formed, and the sergeant, on foot, led it away through the smog. He guided the cars for two miles. Then the bad air became too much for him. He began to gag and to choke on his own mucus. He had to leave them where they were and return to his patrol car—another two-mile walk through the poisoned air.

Members of the force sometimes were called on to perform unusual tasks. Until the growing thickness of the smog and the approach of darkness forced the last patrol cars off the streets, the police helped numerous doctors and midwives visit patients whom they otherwise couldn't have reached. The special 250-man Thames River contingent tied up their boats and did "fog patrol" on foot along the shore. All 250 were excellent swimmers and qualified lifeguards, a fact which probably gave rise to an erroneous report that they rescued a number of people from drowning. They did not; neither did they wear Mae West jackets during the smog nor lose their way and fall into the water.

As the weather grew worse, the London underworld decided to take a holiday. Criminal activity was limited to a few handbag snatchings, some simple burglaries, and an occasional smash-and-grab attack on a small jewelry shop or radio store. Not a single major crime was reported, and the men on duty in the Information Room at Scotland Yard found their work generally slack. The professional criminal needed a car to make his getaway, and he knew that he could not hope to operate a vehicle efficiently with the streets in their present deplorable condition. Contrary to the theories of the immortal Sherlock Holmes, a fogbound metropolis did not prove an open invitation to the underworld, and during the great killer smog there was not the slightest sign of a massive crime wave.

If criminal activity in London was sharply diminishing, though, sickness and death in the city clearly were not. Individual police officers realized, as early as Saturday, that the smog was claiming an exceptionally large number of victims. An officer in Paddington found that ten people in his borough had died "in police circumstances," instead of the expected one or two. In St. Pancras, another officer found sixteen dead instead of five, and the pattern was being repeated in every borough throughout Greater London.

People began coming to their local police stations on Saturday to report that a neighbor was missing.

"Old Mrs. Smith," they would say, "didn't go out to do her shopping, either today or yesterday."

"Mr. Jones, he lives next door, you know—well, he just isn't around."

An officer would accompany them to the address in question and find the body.

Most of the dead who came to the attention of the police were elderly working-class people, living alone. When the smog penetrated their drafty, furnished rooms, they had no one to summon a doctor for them, and they quickly succumbed. No subsequent report would ever touch on the point, but many London policemen knew, from their own experiences, that when the smog came down, anyone poor, sickly, and alone was extremely vulnerable.

There were others in the city who knew, as early as Saturday, that sickness and death were on the rise. The Emergency Bed Service, in its building near London Bridge, was under growing pressure to find hospital space for victims of the smog. More and more doctors were calling the Service, and the twelve women members of each operations team had scarcely a moment's respite, from the time they settled at their posts until the time when their watch was over and they were relieved.

Conditions on Saturday, however, were not yet critical at the Service, and the warning system was not yet in effect. A "white" warning would go out to the appropriate hospital authority only if the percentage of hospital admissions to applications fell below 85 percent. Such a step would serve as a precautionary signal—saying that the Bed Service was hard-pressed and might find itself in serious trouble in a day or two should current trends continue. At 80 percent, a "yellow" warning would go out, and at 75 percent, a "red" one. These would be urgent calls for help; they would say that the situation was very serious, that the resources of the E.B.S. were being rapidly exhausted, and that for one patient in five—or four—no bed could be found.

In response to these warnings, the regional hospital boards would take emergency measures. Admissions from waiting lists would be reduced, extra beds added, and other steps taken to increase accommodations.

At least on Saturday, although the Operations Room was alive with calls, there was no acute emergency. But the senior staff members remained on the alert. Years of experience told them that in a heavy and prolonged fog, it sometimes took three or four days before hospital beds filled up and the sick and the dying had no place to go.

The London Ambulance Service had been operating from 6 General and 21 Accident Stations with increasing difficulty ever since Friday afternoon. Even by then the calls had already mounted far above normal, and poor visibility was making the work of drivers and attendants extremely slow and hazardous. Realizing how critical the situation was becoming, the staff at ambulance headquarters had appealed through the BBC for all off-duty personnel to return to their stations. Dozens of men and women had responded, and as a result, on Friday evening, 22 extra ambulances were kept available, in addition to the normal nighttime complement of 29. On Saturday, the radio appeal was repeated, and 28 extra vehicles were placed in operation.

Morale was extremely high among the Ambulance personnel. Several men and women on sick leave returned promptly to duty; many drivers put on white coats and left their stations to walk ahead of a vehicle that had no attendant and that otherwise could not have gone out to answer calls. Operating without radios, each ambulance crew was entirely on its own, from departure to return, save when a driver was able to reach a telephone to check in, and this lack of communication made the general task more difficult for all concerned.

Drivers and attendants performed many prodigies of service as the smog grew worse. In the western part of the city, two drivers, alternating on the road and behind the wheel, traveled 14 miles to bring an acute mastoid patient to a hospital. It was by no means the most arduous trip undertaken. Numerous members of the Service returned to their stations utterly exhausted, after walking 15 or 20 miles on a call. By then, their eyes were streaming, they were sick to their stomachs, and their throbbing, blistered feet were covered with blood. Drivers and attendants, too weary to go out again, stayed in their stations, caught a few hours' sleep, and then returned to the job.

Day and night, driving and carrying flares, caring for the sick, the crews of the Ambulance Service answered the endless flood of calls; it seemed hard to believe that things could become worse than they already were on the second full day of the killer smog.

Twenty-seven

AS THE HOURS passed on Saturday, Dr. Williston became more and more certain that his own borough, in fact the entire city of London, was experiencing an air pollution disaster. There were all kinds of portents. Traveling to work, he coughed and hawked and spat black mucus a dozen times into his handkerchief. When he reached the Health Department his smarting eyes were streaming tears.

Most staff members came in late. Some had merely run into delays finding transportation. A number had been sick during the previous evening until vomiting had relieved them and, now, feeling better after a night's rest, they had decided to struggle back to the job. And then there were a few who didn't arrive at all.

Dr. Williston heard countless rumors as he made his rounds. He talked with several sanitary inspectors, men who were familiar with every street and house in the borough. Because they spent so much of their time outside the office, they often knew a great deal about what was going on. The old people, the inspectors told him, were sick, and so were some of the very young children. That was to be expected in a fog. But things weren't stopping there. Others were being affected, too—the middle-aged and even people in their twenties and thirties. In almost every block you ran into a story about someone who hadn't been seen for the last couple of days, an old man or woman who hadn't shown up at their usual haunts. A familiar face was missed at the greengrocer, the butcher, the tobacconist. And another thing—most of the doctors in the borough seemed to be exceptionally busy, not to mention the two ambulances that had been seen driving by the Health Department in the space of an hour.

Before lunch, Dr. Williston glanced out of his office window and watched young Amberson, a wraithlike figure through the mist, bending over to repair a tire. The garageman had probably been there all morning. No doubt the car's owner had insisted that his tire be fixed on time, even though he would have no place to drive to until the weather cleared.

And then, during the afternoon, a telephone inquiry came from a news reporter. Dr. Williston never learned—for he didn't ask—how the reporter first happened to hear about him. He guessed that the newsman had called County Hall and that a spokesman there had mentioned the Borough M.O.H. who believed that London was facing a possible calamity.

Dr. Williston said yes, he certainly thought that there was a temperature inversion at present. He felt quite certain that this was anything but an ordinary winter's fog. In his opinion—and he did not in the least mind being quoted—it was like Donora, Pennsylvania, or the Meuse valley in Belgium, a poisonous and highly dangerous smog that posed a serious threat to the health of everyone in the city.

There were many inquiries after that. For a time, his office phone never seemed to stop ringing. The calls came from other newsmen and always with the same questions: "Is something going on in the city? Is the air outside really a menace? Should you say that we've got a poisonous smog with us this afternoon?" He replied that he believed so. A smog like Donora, like the Meuse.

When evening came, he left the office to return home. Outside, he held a handkerchief over his nose and mouth. As he turned the first corner, a woman who lived in the neighborhood loomed out of the dark. He could see that she had just come from the house where the Ambersons lived.

Dr. Williston nodded, and the woman halted in front of him. "He's dead," she told him. "Who's dead?"

"Nick Amberson. I've been with Ruth."

"*Dead?* Why, I saw him working only four or five hours ago."

Dr. Williston learned that Amberson had come in at noon and told his wife that his throat was burning. He took a swallow or two of milk but couldn't eat anything more. He complained of feeling tired and said that instead of returning to work, he was going to rest for awhile. His wife had looked into their bedroom around two-thirty. He seemed to be sleeping peacefully. She looked in again at four, thinking it strange that he should still be asleep. She found him quite cold. He had not been under a doctor's care. There had been nothing the matter with him, nothing, at least, that anyone had known about.

Afterward, two problems continued to haunt Dr. Williston for a long time. One was the question of Amberson. What might have happened if he had told the garageman that there was a smog, had cautioned him of the dangers, warned him not to work too long outside? Would he have heeded the advice? And suppose he had—mightn't he have died anyway? Wasn't it possible, even probable, that he had been subject to some undetected disability and that the pretty, red-haired Mrs. Amberson was fated to become a widow from the moment the smog came down?

The other problem concerned the reporters. They had called him, they had asked their questions, and he had told them that a lethal smog very likely had come to the city. But no mention of that possibility appeared in their stories, and no precautionary words were carried on the BBC. Even when the newspapers printed their accounts of the afflicted cattle at Earl's Court, no editor or reporter seemed able to reach the obvious conclusion that if an extraordinary number of farm animals were dying because of the smog, then surely an extraordinary number of human beings might be dying, too.

But no reference to Donora, no reference to the Meuse, ever appeared. It was a baffling problem, and Dr. Williston never did find a satisfactory answer to it.

Nearly all of London's two thousand general practitioners were kept extremely busy on Saturday, and for the few among them who also served as police surgeons, the way Dr. Geoffrey Roberts did, there was no letup in work from early morning until long after dark.

Some of the people Dr. Roberts saw were his own patients; some were the men and women whom the police called him about and asked him to visit. It wasn't an easy or a pleasant task to reach them. It meant moving constantly about through the dank, windless streets, wiping your eyes and breathing in the frigid, choking air. He found that he rarely could see more than three or four yards ahead, and often the distance was less. The other side of the street was never visible. Oddly enough, the air at ground level, to a height of about two or three feet—up as far as your knees—was usually clear. Above that, there was the dense, impenetrable mist.

The cars and buses crawled along in low gear, and in the clear air near the ground, he often could see their exhausts, pouring out fumes. Sometimes, when a bus started up, it left behind furious eddies of swirling, yellow fog.

The atmosphere was becoming smokier and more sulfurous, almost unbearably so. Even the Underground was a trial, for the foul air had seeped into the tunnels and stations, and the passage of the trains could not dispel it.

There were curious sights to be seen at times. While standing on one station platform, the doctor observed a most unlikely couple emerge from the stairwell. They were a young bride and groom, dressed for their wedding.

Dr. Roberts approached and had a chat with them. They'd just gotten married a few minutes before. Now they were on their way to the reception. They had decided to take the Underground, the groom explained, because there weren't any taxis left in the streets, and there hadn't been any other way for them to get there.

The young bride was happy, but rather rueful about one thing. Her wedding dress, she indicated to Dr. Roberts, was no longer very clean. He saw that the smog had turned it nearly black, for they had been compelled to walk a considerable distance, about a quarter of a mile, from the church to the Underground station. The groom pointed out though that "dirty or not" made very little difference now, since she had gotten herself a husband and wouldn't be needing the wedding dress for some time to come. Soon the bridal couple forgot that he was even there. Dr. Roberts was pleased with the sight of two such happy faces. He didn't find many others that day in the smog.

Morning and evening, he made his way around the borough, seeing his own cases, answering calls from the police, until sickness and death became a familiar presence.

There was Beatrice Weller, 76, in poor health and chesty. She was a solitary old woman, who kept to herself. Her landlady found her dead in her narrow bed.

There was Ernest Clapp, 75, arthritic and chesty, who was suffering a coronary occlusion as Dr. Roberts arrived. He sent for an ambulance, but there was a delay of an hour and a half, and Clapp was moribund by the time it came.

There was Arthur Payson, 64, an asthmatic since being gassed during World War I. He lived in an attic and spent much of his time in bed. He had been sick a week before the fog had begun. He had complained about the weather on Friday. Now, on Saturday, he was dead.

There was Jane Ogden, a widow, aged 62. She'd always been chesty, but ir good general health. Several days before the fog, she'd had a mild touch of bronchitis. She'd been up and about on Friday and again this morning, Saturday, when she'd complained of feeling a bit tired and depressed but nothing more. She hadn't really been "bothered" by the fog this time, the way she usually was. The end had come very suddenly, according to her friend, the one who'd found her, sitting up, dead in her chair.

It was long after nightfall before Dr. Roberts had answered the last of his calls and could return to his house for a bite of supper and a few hours' sleep. By then, he had thought several times of his conversation the previous day with Dr. Williston, the Borough M.O.H. Something certainly was "going on" in London. The old and the sick, and possibly many others besides, were being carried off in large numbers. He couldn't help but wonder how bad it really was. Had all the other boroughs been equally affected? Were people dying in the suburbs, too?

And of course the real question was: When would the fog lift? For if it didn't very soon, there were any number of other patients he'd seen who weren't going to survive either.

On Saturday night, the smog grew even more dense and contaminated. Visibility at both Kew and Kingsway was nil.

The air was almost completely calm. At Kew, a velocity of one knot was recorded. No wind at all could be measured at Kingsway, and none had been measured there for 42 hours.

The high-pressure anticyclone remained immobile; its center was still directly above the Thames valley, and the thermal inversion w
sealed in complete
choking fumes from
ing at full strength
air—to the people l
estimates made afte
were four and five ti
in borough after bc

The late weath
cern. "The official
said, "is that over m
fog and frost will be
persist near large tc
periods after midmc
cold."

There was no r
But the toll was gro
the death rate in Greater London had more than doubled.

Ch 27

· City of London - Air P
disaster
Been followed of the fog

· Rate of deaths (x2)

Twenty-eight

SUNDAY'S DAWN was damp and bitterly cold. There was still no wind. Clouds of polluted fog choked the streets, pressed against windowpanes, blotted out the sun. Grayish streaks of fog hung inside all but the most tightly sealed rooms, until the heat from a freshly lit gas or coal fire could dispel them.

By Sunday morning, London's housewives had discovered that the invading smog left a thick, black, sticky film on almost everything it touched. It tarnished metal badly; it soiled curtains and furniture covers so thoroughly that no amount of scrubbing seemed likely to restore the materials to their original colors or brightness.

Out-of-doors, conditions were even worse than the previous day. No ships moved on the Thames. The airports were still shut down. Distant and local trains were running an hour or two late, and some were not running at all. Cancellation and delay meant a reduction in food deliveries to the beleaguered city and, in several boroughs, milk no longer was obtainable. For the first time the Underground was badly affected, with at least one line falling an hour behind schedule. During the night, the Ambulance Service had issued another radio appeal for off-duty drivers to return to their stations, and enough of them had reported so that 20 additional vehicles could be sent out to answer calls. The Postal Service had declared an emergency, with all available personnel remaining on the job to keep the mail sacks moving.

As daylight came, buses and motor coaches emerged from their depots, with conductors walking resolutely ahead carrying flares. Soon most of the vehicles either were completely lost in the smog or were tied up in traffic. By noon, many of them were crawling back toward their home garages, the drivers convinced that there simply was no getting through.

Despite renewed warnings from the Automobile Association, a number of inveterate drivers attempted to enter the city. Their efforts met with little success, and as the morning wore on, the control room at Fanum House again found itself swamped with pleas for assistance. But this time the smog was too thick for even the A.A. rescue service. The vans could not reach most of the stranded motorists, and still more cars were abandoned. Before long, numerous streets became so littered that they resembled parts of a foggy battlefield.

The men at Fanum House were grateful it was Sunday. Had the thickest part of the smog come on a weekday, the chaos would have been even more extensive. As it was, driving conditions in London had never been worse.

Mrs. Wilcox awoke when it grew light on Sunday. Her head was pounding as if an endless succession of broad steel nails were being hammered into her skull. The migraine she had suffered for years hadn't prepared her for such agony. And when she tried to breathe, new waves of pain spread across her chest; and it felt as if her lungs were being squeezed out through her ribs.

Somehow she managed to make herself heard down the hall. When her niece came in, she gasped, "Call Speyer."

The doctor came from his house in South Norwood as quickly as he could, not by car as he usually did, but on foot, a half-dozen twisting blocks through the dense morning smog. When she saw him she whispered, "My head, my head. Do something for my head."

Dr. Speyer gave her an injection, and little by little the unbearable pains began to subside. Vaguely, as if in a dream, she realized that Harold had come into the room with some new medicine that the doctor had sent him out to get at the chemist's.

He and the doctor raised her up in the bed so that she could swallow one of the pills to help her breathing. She got it down, and later, she didn't know when, the pains in her chest grew easier, too, and she was able to draw in some air again, to fill up her lungs.

Dr. Speyer waited in the house until Mrs. Wilcox finally fell into a doze. Then he closed his black bag and went downstairs. While putting on his coat, he told Amy that he would be back in the afternoon and that for awhile he would be coming in twice a day.

It had been a near thing that morning, and her aunt was still far from out of the woods. In all probability, the pains in her head and chest had been the result of a severe oxygen deficiency. Because of her bronchitis, she hadn't been able to take in enough to meet her bodily needs. By the time they had summoned him, her aunt had been strangling to death for lack of air.

The doctor cautioned her not to leave the patient alone in her room. "Someone," he said, "must be in there with her at all times." When asked what he believed Mrs. Wilcox's chances were, he replied that since there was no evidence of any heart involvement, he thought they might even run as high as 50 percent.

On Sunday, Mary Chapman called the doctor, and he visited the house in Little Stanmore later in the morning. The baby *was* sick—it hadn't been merely her imagination. His breathing was distinctly wheezy. John, her father and mother, everyone noticed it now, and they all said that she had been right to think Albert unwell on the previous day.

The doctor was reassuring, even though he told her little that she hadn't known before. It was an encouraging sign, he said, that the baby's fever was very slight. Breathing was a bit restricted, and the fog was unquestionably affecting him, but once it had lifted he would most certainly recover completely in a very short time.

In Putney, a neighbor appeared quite early in the morning and told Mrs. Shelton that she'd better come round to her father-in-law's without delay. When she arrived, the old gentleman had just gotten over a heart seizure and was still suffering severe abdominal pains. She gave him his usual medicine, and soon he did say that he felt a little better.

She sat with him all morning. His breathing remained heavy, but he was fully conscious. He spoke to her several times. Whenever she moved around the room, he followed her with his eyes.

Just before noon the doctor came and examined him. The patient's heart was affected, he said. Mrs. Shelton went to the chemist's to get some tablets for his breathing and some drops for his heart. When she returned and gave him the new medicine he seemed to improve a bit. He said that the pain was growing easier.

But he could eat no solid food, just a few sips of milk or tea mixed with some brandy. She saw that he was gradually getting weaker. In another hour or so he no longer had the strength to pump the inhaler by himself, and whenever he said that he needed it, she had to work it for him.

Mrs. Shelton knew it was the fog that was finishing him. It was awful out-of-doors, worse than she'd ever seen it. And of course some had gotten inside the room. She couldn't help but think that if such a bad fog hadn't come, her father-in-law might easily have lived for another year or two. And she couldn't help but wonder how much longer the deathwatch was likely to last.

Even on Sunday, as the pollution in Greater London reached staggering proportions, there were still a few isolated places in the capital where the atmosphere remained fresh and clean. On the hills of the city, above the incredibly low ceiling of smog, there was bright winter sunlight; visibility was normal, and a steady, wholesome breeze was stirring the air. Shooter's Hill, at an elevation of 400 feet, was clear all during the day. So were the upper slopes of Hampstead Heath, which rose to an equal height, and Wimbledon Common, a mere 150 to 200 feet above sea level. Local residents who came out on these modest hills could look down on the lower parts of fogbound London and be reminded of beautifully illustrated fairy tales or the romantic legends of the lost cities of Atlantis and Avalon. The capital—if you only could get high enough—was actually quite an agreeable place for a mid-Sunday stroll.

But below the hills and the lid of the inversion, conditions continued to deteriorate throughout the afternoon. The smog thickened, hour by hour, becoming increasingly foul and lethal. Visibility of more than a yard or two was rare. The switchboard at Fanum House was still swamped with calls for assistance, but now the Automobile Association's rescue vans no longer were even attempting to get through. Eventually, the last private cars were abandoned on the darkened streets, and their drivers disappeared on foot into the murk. At ten o'clock, London Transport was forced to announce that all buses, except for a few on three routes in the extreme southern portion of the city, were out of operation. By then, there was scarcely a vehicle moving in all of London.

During the evening hours, the Ambulance Service was in a shambles. Drivers and attendants were approaching physical exhaustion; supplies of flares were running out; often it took six or eight hours for a new supply to reach the requesting station.

As driving conditions worsened, the average time of an ambulance trip to hospital increased from a normal thirty or forty minutes to well over two hours. It became evident that extraordinary measures would have to be put into effect. Instead of carrying only a single patient, the overworked crews were authorized to carry two, and then, in more desperate circumstances, even three or four patients on each trip.

Near London Bridge, the Emergency Bed Service was receiving a mounting number of calls from the city's doctors. But at many hospitals, facilities were already filled, and the time clearly was coming when at least one out of every five patients referred to the E.B.S. would no longer find an accommodation. On Sunday night, as the danger point drew near, the Service prepared to issue its first-stage "white" warning.

By then, a new sort of inquiry was beginning to be received from various hospitals around London—the hospital had agreed to accept a patient, but the patient had not yet arrived. Did the E.B.S., by any chance, know where the overdue ambulance might be?

Frequently, the Bed Service did not. No ambulance carried a radio, and so the Duty Crew near London Bridge was out of contact with all vehicles from the time they left their stations till the time they arrived.

At about nine o'clock on Sunday night, the Bed Service arranged for an ambulance to transport four patients to a hospital in the north still had not been deli reason. Where *were* th

A member of the ambulance station, bu He was missing, indee

The member of t and this time the mys out, had not arrived a More than an hour ar while still en route, h that the last of thei died. The driver was swung past the hosp dead passengers to th

Ch 28

· No wind

· Hospital waits were then over 2 hrs

· Delivered 4 dead passengers

Twenty-nine

Dr. Geoffrey Roberts worked from early dawn until long after dark on Sunday, as did most of the city's physicians. He visited the sick and the dying, wrote out prescriptions, examined the dead.

Some of the smog victims were his own patients; some were complete strangers. He had never seen Elizabeth Farmer before. She was the widow of a railway laborer—a thin, wrinkled old woman of 83. She had suffered from chronic bronchitis "for some years," according to her landlady. The fog had made her much worse. The landlady had found her, lying in her bed, early on Sunday morning—"the first thing after my breakfast." Judging by the condition of the body, she must have died between midnight and 4:00 or 5:00 A.M.

Annie Nelson was neither old nor a stranger. Dr. Roberts had been treating her for several years. She was a blond, delicate child of eleven, generally unwell. Every winter she had a bout of bronchitis. He'd suspected that there was something more seriously amiss, possibly tuberculosis, and was going to recommend tests in the spring. On Friday, the beginning of the fog, he had visited the girl. Saturday afternoon he had paid another call. She was having trouble breathing. Her father met him at the front door on Sunday. Annie had died during the night. They hadn't thought to phone him because there hadn't seemed to be any need to. One moment she was sleeping quietly—the next she was gone.

Floyd Carter, a licensed victualler's potman, was found dead in the street near the hotel where he had worked for the past twelve years. His sister told Dr. Roberts that he had had high blood pressure but no heart trouble that she knew of. He had been an extremely heavy smoker, though, and she believed that a doctor had warned him at one time that it might be having a detrimental effect on his heart. He had complained about his breathing on Saturday, but his sister, a small woman with a sparrowlike face, said *she* was sure it was all the smoking. She herself didn't approve of smoking. As far as Dr. Roberts could tell on such brief acquaintance, the evils of tobacco were of more concern to her than her brother's untimely "passing on."

He didn't see his patient Valerie Todd on Sunday. Mrs. Todd was 36 and had suffered from asthma for several years. She had come down with a mild cold before the fog, and her husband had called him in to see her on Tuesday. Her condition did not appear serious. As late as Friday she seemed to be making a normal recovery. But on Saturday he found her delirious. She was having a great deal of difficulty breathing. He ordered her immediate removal to hospital. Unfortunately, she had been forced to remain in the ambulance for two and a half hours because of the fog. Before he could visit her on Sunday, he received a message that she was dead.

After he had made his last call, Dr. Roberts returned home, through the cold, foggy night. While cooking a solitary supper, he had a chance to look back at the past three days, to recall some of the things that people had been telling him, and to sort out some of his own impressions as well.

For anyone whose health had not been affected, the worst thing about the weather outside did not seem to be the obvious unpleasantness that came from breathing dirty air, nor the extraordinary inconvenience of walking about through an opaque fog, but rather the emotional strain that came on you when you made your way along the streets, always alone. It was this sense of isolation, of being completely apart from everyone else, that somehow made you fearful—though fearful of precisely what, you really couldn't say, not even after you realized that you *were* afraid.

Those who'd managed to remain indoors seemed equally affected. Many were quite evidently on edge. Some mentioned the constant physical *presence* of the fog, the way it appeared to surround them, to cut them off from other people and from everyday, familiar sights. And, of course, for anyone who had been made sick by a previous fog, the mere sight of another one now was simply terrifying.

He had talked with a number of chest patients about their thoughts and sensations, and he remembered the words of one articulate old man, who said that the worst part of a fog was the burning in your throat. . . . "It makes you feel certain that you're going to die, that death is surely coming for you, partly because of your difficulty in breathing and partly because of the fierce pain in your throat and lungs, which makes the flesh itself seem on fire . . . and adding to your terror is the *sight* of the fog, when you see it there all around you, like some kind of gray, obscene animal, outside your window, drifting, floating, almost looking in at you, as though it were waiting there to claim you, to seize you, to choke you . . . to squeeze the breath, the very life out of your body. . . ."

Dr. Roberts went to bed early in the hope of getting a good night's rest. But he wasn't surprised when the telephone rang just before eleven. It was a patient saying that his son, a boy of eight, had a bad sore throat. The lad seemed feverish, had difficulty swallowing, couldn't sleep. Maybe it was the flu—or something worse.

Wearily, Dr. Roberts got dressed again and let himself out into the pitch-black night. It was just under a mile to the boy's house. The best way to get there would be on the Underground. Perhaps the only way. He began to walk toward the nearest station, three blocks off.

The fog was unbelievably dense. At times he could hold his arm straight out in front of him and actually lose sight of his own fingers. The city seemed completely deserted. No traffic moved in the streets, no pedestrians on the pavements. The air was a dead calm, not the least breath of wind stirring. And not a sound anywhere, except far, far away, an occasional foghorn could be heard on one of the small ships tied up somewhere along the Thames—an incredible stillness, an awesome sense of being absolutely alone.

He lost his way, which wasn't really surprising—lost it so completely that after awhile he gave up any hope of finding the entrance to the Underground. He continued to wander about, never knowing where he might be, never seeing a single, recognizable landmark. For hours, literally for hours. And even a landmark of some kind would have been of little use because five feet from a familiar spot, you were back in the fog and utterly lost again.

It was after one o'clock when he finally realized where he was standing. He had done exactly what people were supposed to do in a dense fog. The classic, instinctual procedure —he had wandered in a huge, irregular circle, until at last his errant footsteps had brought him back home.

Dr. Roberts began to think that there was no way he could reach his patient. In the fog you were like a blind man, you could grope about all night, without a chance of keeping yourself straight, or of ever finding—

Like a blind man? Now hold on a bit—what about

someone like Duncan Hunter, the blind patient who had come to his office the other day? The heaviest fog would mean nothing to him because he already was accustomed to walking through the streets without using his eyes, without ever seeing where he was going. Maybe a blind man was the only one who *could* get about in such a dense fog.

Both Hunter and his wife were very good sports about it, when he got them up out of bed and explained the problem. Mrs. Hunter made coffee and sandwiches while her husband dressed. After they'd eaten, they set out together, he and his blind neighbor, just before two o'clock, to have another try at reaching the lad who was sick.

It was the strangest journey that he'd ever taken. Everything seemed entirely reversed. Duncan Hunter moved ahead confidently with his cane, either tapping it on the sidewalk or swinging it from side to side in a long sweeping motion to make sure that there were no obstacles in their path. When they came to a curb, it was Hunter who sensed it, and said, "Here's another, I think . . . all right, careful now, Doctor, just a short step down."

As for himself, there was blindness, hesitation, until finally, in a perfect reversal of roles, he took his companion's arm, and Hunter began to steer him along, and—one had to confess it—he felt extremely grateful for the blind man's assistance.

They made the trip in very good time, though Hunter said they could have done much better if there had been at least a few vehicles moving along the streets. He missed the ordinary sounds of traffic. He always used them in getting about—most blind people did. Now he had to stop every once in awhile and shout. The answering echoes were helpful. They took the place of passing vehicles and told him where they were.

They reached the house not long after three. The boy had a fever of 101, and his throat showed signs of a possible strep infection. There was no problem in treating him. Dr. Roberts promised to come in again the next afternoon, and then he and Hunter stepped into the fog again.

Their return went off without a hitch. Perfectly. His companion tapping and sweeping the cane, both of them shouting and then listening for the echoes—Dr. Roberts and his singular guide, walking confidently through the darkest hours of the night.

And when they got back home, Duncan Hunter said that he was happy to have been of service. "In a real fog," he added with a grin, "it's sometimes handy to know a blind man, wouldn't you say?"

≡

By the time that Sunday, the third full day of the killer smog was over, the amount of pollution in London's air had reached astronomical heights. Yet afterward, no one could say with any degree of certainty how bad things actually had been. The official estimate was that at widely separated "individual sites" the maximum concentration of smoke had ranged between three and ten times the amount usually found in Greater London's dirty and unwholesome winter air. The amount of sulfur dioxide was said to have been from three to twelve times normal.

But these figures had a limited significance. During the worst of the smog, at least some of the official readings had been made on instruments that were no longer functioning. The matter was put quite clearly by one borough official, in his annual report, when he said, "the pollution was so heavy that our instruments were incapable of measuring the quantity," a fact not subsequently disclosed in the official survey produced for the government by the Ministry of Health.

Perhaps the most valid assessment of the amount of pollution in the city's air was made in a most unlikely quarter —the National Gallery, Trafalgar Square. Apparently, no reporter or health official discovered this interesting source of information. To the National Smoke Abatement Society belonged the sole credit for soliciting and publishing a brief communication from the Ministry of Works concerning the air-conditioning plant the Ministry had installed in the gallery a month before the advent of the smog.

"The air-conditioning plant," the letter stated, "has been operating on its present duties since mid-November, 1952. We have, as a normal check, recorded the filter resistance in a daily log sheet.

"From these records it would seem that in the course of 24 hours of fog, the filters clogged at a rate 26 times the normal, and in one period of four hours the rate was 54 times the normal."

Whether there had been actually 12, or 26, or 54 times as much smoke in London's air as on an average winter's day, made no critical difference—the effect of the pollution, however great, was incontrovertible. The death rate in Greater London, on Sunday, December 7, was four times higher than it had been on the previous Sunday, and the city was suffering a calamity almost unparalleled in its modern history.

As one medical journal said, "In the past hundred years only the peak week of the influenza pandemic in November, 1918, produced more deaths over the expected normal than did the man-made fog. . . . Even the cholera epidemic of 1866 could not quite equal it."

Thirty

ON MONDAY, December 8, just before dawn, the anticyclone finally began to edge forward again, on a course that ultimately would carry it away from London and the valley of the Thames. Behind it, the mass of low-pressure air continued to advance; crossing Scotland and northern England, it brought with it warmer temperatures, periods of light rain, and the promise of an eventual end to the smog.

By daylight, a faint breeze stirred in the capital for the first time in almost a hundred hours. The long-range weather outlook now appeared somewhat brighter; the BBC's early forecast, while calling for another foggy morning in Greater London, added that there were definite grounds for expecting a general improvement, either during the late afternoon or early evening.

In the meantime, although conditions varied considerably from place to place and from hour to hour, the smog continued to plague the city, much as it had before. All forms of transportation were still heavily affected. No Green Line coaches entered central London; suburban and long-distance trains reported delays of an hour or more on many lines, and there were frequent cancellations. The Thames remained fogbound, with no ships moving; during the morning, London Airport was closed to all flights. The Underground ran as much as 15 minutes late, due to the difficulty experienced by engineers and other personnel in reaching work and to the extra passengers the overloaded trains had to carry.

Driving conditions were still chaotic. London Transport put many of its buses back into service to meet the demands of the weekday rush hour, and soon there were new traffic snarls at Hyde Park Corner, Piccadilly Circus, Trafalgar Square, and the Broadway, Hammersmith. In some areas, where the smog became thinner and even the sun appeared briefly, the police attempted to help motorists retrieve the cars they had abandoned on Saturday and Sunday; but before long the smog closed down again, and most of the cars remained there unclaimed, clogging the streets of the city.

The Ambulance Service struggled on with extra crews of off-duty drivers and attendants answering yet another call for volunteers. The Emergency Bed Service, its ability to find hospital accommodations now seriously reduced, issued its preliminary "white" warning at 11:00 A.M.

For the first time the people of Great Britain could read generous accounts of the killer smog in their daily papers, accounts that were more distinguished for their imaginative qualities than for their accuracy. *The Times* emphasized the breakdown that had occurred in public transport, and then, entering a realm of journalistic fantasy, described the supposedly "widespread" activities of housebreakers, as well as the "large" number of people who had been attacked on the streets.

The paper did not suggest, however, that a disaster might have been taking place in the capital. The smog, according to *The Times*, had "caused a crop of minor accidents on the roads," and apparently it had been these which had kept the Ambulance Service on a full-time emergency footing during the entire weekend. No mention was made of human illness or fatalities, but an item did note that some of the prime cattle at the Smithfield show had contracted respiratory troubles "either on their long journeys or in the hall." The first casualty at Earl's Court was reported—an Aberdeen-Angus entry.

The *Manchester Guardian* headlined its summary "Third Day of a London Particular" and stressed railway delays, minor road accidents, and crime.

The tabloid *Daily Mirror* began on a fiscal note, stating that "the great smog blanket" was costing the nation an estimated two million pounds a day in lost goods and services. The rest of its coverage was remarkable for several stunning flights of fancy. One story contained a bogus description of London-in-flames, of fires which had "blazed unchecked while brigades groped through the thick murk." Another, devoted to conditions along the river, stated that "Danger lurked on the docks, where at least eight persons missed the quay-sides—and stepped over. Dock patrols wore life jackets—just in case." And finally, a disease called "fog fever" was reported to have "hit cattle worth thousands of pounds at Earl's Court."

Either the newspaper staff did not suspect that "fog fever" might also have "hit" people, or else it kept its suspicions to itself.

The *Edinburgh Evening News* did slightly better—but only slightly. Its story was headlined: "Big Crime Wave Hits London While Fog Lasted." Farther down its three-column spread, the paper disclosed that by now eight cattle at Earl's Court either had died or had been slaughtered at the request of their owners to put the suffering animals out of their misery. Penicillin and whiskey-soaked rags, held over the animals' nostrils, had reputedly saved the rest.

And then, at the very tag-end of its story, the Edinburgh paper printed a statement from the National Smoke Abatement Society: "Our lack of progress in abolishing smoke is shown by history repeating itself at the Smithfield Cattle Show. As long ago as 1873, the show coincided with severe fog and many beasts died or had to be slaughtered. The human death-rate from respiratory diseases also rose sharply, as it usually does after intense smoke fog."

The *Edinburgh Evening News* did not choose to add a comment of its own, and there its description of the killer smog ended.

Meanwhile, undiscovered by the press and radio, thousands of Londoners continued to struggle for air—and life—throughout the fourth day of the smog. In Stepney, Mrs. Shelton never left her father-in-law's side. About one in the morning he had sat up in bed and clutched his stomach. He said that he had a bad pain there. The heart attacks lasted for about an hour and a half and seemed to rob him of his last strength. When they were done, he was very weak and in a cold sweat. Between the spasms, she worked his inhaler for him so he could breathe more easily. Finally the pains passed away, and he lay back exhausted.

After that he did not want anything except his inhaler. When he needed it, he signaled with his hand, because it was too much effort to speak.

At 5:30 A.M. Mrs. Shelton told him that the fog outside was clearing a little and that she could see the traffic lights up the road again. "That's good," he said.

"Perhaps you'll feel a bit better now, Father." He nodded and settled down in the bed. His eyes were fixed and half-open. He did not move his arms out of the bedclothes, and when she spoke to him, he no longer answered. She could tell by the whiteness of his face that the end was near. She hoped that he would speak again, but he didn't.

She went out and got a neighbor to keep watch and went to fetch the doctor, but by the time they returned it was too late. He had "just gone." The morning was a bit lighter, but the fog was still thick as she walked back home.

Dr. Speyer came to visit Mrs. Wilcox twice on Monday, in the morning and again in the evening. Her niece Amy didn't have to be told how worried the doctor was. Her aunt was holding her own, but no more than that. The doctor said he expected her breathing to improve as soon as the fog was over. What might happen then he didn't know. Heart or lungs—there *could* be complications. And Amy was to be absolutely sure, in the meantime, that somebody stayed with Mrs. Wilcox, every minute, around the clock.

The fog remained thick, all of Monday, in Little Stanmore. The doctor came as he had promised, but this time Mary Chapman found no comfort in his words.

Albert's wheeze was worse than ever, or so it seemed to her. He looked so small and vulnerable lying in his crib, trying to get more air through his tiny nose and mouth, down into his chest.

The doctor agreed that there *had* been no improvement but told her that once the fog lifted—and the weather report said it was only a matter of a few hours more—why, her baby was likely to come around very quickly, indeed.

And yet, for some reason, she just didn't believe the doctor anymore. When John came in that night, on his way back from work, she told him so. For the first time she felt that something awful might be going to happen. And what was even worse—there was nothing that she or anybody else could do to keep it from happening.

Angela Burke went ahead and had it done on Monday. Fog or no fog, she just decided in the morning that she couldn't wait any longer. So, during her lunch hour, she slipped away from school and went to the hairdressers in Marylebone High Street where she had her hair cut short and then set in a permanent wave, like all her friends.

Satisfied, but feeling almost a stranger to herself, she stepped out into the fog again. It was an odd thing—it made you feel very odd to see yourself looking so different, especially all at once. And the worst part of it, of course, still lay ahead. That night, when she went home . . .

It happened to her without warning, as she was walking by the Outer Circle at Regent's Park. She looked up, and there it was, *staring* at her. It made her heart pound.

He was staring down at her, God, with His terrible all-seeing eye. Watching her as she walked about filled with willfulness and pride—the sinful child.

It was absolutely terrifying while it lasted. And then—it was probably only a few seconds later—she knew what it was and could have laughed hysterically at herself for being such an *awful* ninny. It was only the *sun*, a ghastly, copper colored sun, reappearing for the first time in days. Just the sun, trying to break through for a moment . . . but how it had scared her . . . "God in His wrath" . . . wasn't it frightful, the things you couldn't help but believe, in spite of yourself?

And then, later on when she went home, something else almost as queer happened. Her mother took one look and began to cry. Just broke down. *That* she'd never expected. And her dad said very quietly, "I think it looks rather better," and went back behind his newspaper. That she *had* expected. And sometime during the evening, he must have talked with her mother about it. For no more was said. After all that fuss—simply nothing.

One's parents were odd, there was no getting around it.

150 London's doctors worked overtime again on Monday. The air in the city remained massively contaminated, despite the limited improvement in visibility. The number of people sick and dying was still on the rise. Many doctors knew by

nightfall that they had not been called on to toil as hard as this since the worst days of the blitz.

South of the river, Dr. Roberts continued his rounds, fortified by only three or four hours' sleep. His brain seemed to be growing numb with the repetition of grim duties—the sounding of straining lungs and hearts, the prescribing of expectorants and penicillin, the ordering of patients to hospital, the examination of the dead.

One of Monday's cases remained indelibly impressed on his mind. She was an old woman of 75, the widow of a postman. Her name was Ruth Moss; she lived alone, in a narrow, bare, cramped room, overlooking a dark street. She was often sick with bronchitis, according to her friend who lived next door.

On Saturday, Mrs. Moss's friend had been away visiting a married daughter. Alone in the fog Mrs. Moss had felt the end coming. She had written her friend a note. It said that she was already sick and that the weather was growing worse. The fog was inside her room. She had a box of keepsakes in her closet, and she wanted her friend to please send them on to a cousin of hers in Devon.

The last line of the note said, "I think this fog will kill me."

Looking down at the bed, Dr. Roberts couldn't help but wonder how many other desperate souls must have thought that selfsame thing at some dark and terrible hour of the night.

≈

Early Monday evening, the center of the anticyclone finally moved off to the east, away from London. But the back edge of the cold air mass hung over the city, and the temperature inversion was still unbroken. The earlier weather predictions had been premature; the smog did not lift. Instead, as nightfall came, it thickened once more, reducing visibility to a yard or less in many parts of the metropolis.

Again there were large traffic tie-ups, and bus services were sharply curtailed. At Stratford, in East London, all double-deckers were taken off; a queue of three thousand people soon formed outside the Underground station, and the police had to dispatch extra constables to control the crowds waiting to reach the ticket office window.

Shipping remained completely paralyzed on the Thames. Conditions were little better at London Airport, which had been open briefly during midafternoon. Only two planes had left, one bound for New York, and one for West Africa. Four planes had managed to land. By early evening, Heathrow was fogged in again, and all incoming flights were being directed to fields that lay beyond the contaminated area.

Monday night was damp and cold, and power stations, working at full capacity to provide the city with heat and light, continued to pour smoke and sulfur dioxide from their chimney stacks. London's two hundred general hospitals, crowded with patients, added more pollution to the atmosphere from their glowing furnaces—poisoning the air of the smog victims while warming their rooms.

No mention of human illness marred the serenity of the BBC's evening news broadcasts, though it was reported that the number of fatalities among the prize cattle at Earl's Court had now risen to eleven.

Originally, the 6:00 P.M. broadcast had contained this note of warning: "The National Smoke Abatement Society says that the fog was the dirtiest in London for many years and shows that smoke from coal-burning domestic fires remains a serious menace." But listeners did not hear the item, for it was deleted from the broadcast by a member of the staff.

During the evening the smog invaded a number of movie houses around Leicester Square, where patrons complained that they couldn't see what was happening on the screen. Many left early and demanded their money back.

The smog was heavy at Sadler's Wells, obscuring the stage and making the singers' task of performing *La Traviata* extremely difficult. The audience coughed incessantly, too, and the performance was canceled after a single act. With its fatally stricken, tubercular heroine, the Verdi opera had been an appropriate selection for the last night of the disaster.

By the time that Monday, December 8, was over, the death rate in Greater London had finally reached its peak. Five or six hundred people had perished from the smog during the past twenty-four hours alone. Between fifteen hundred and two thousand had been killed since Friday morning, and at least an equal number were fated to die within the next two weeks. Tens of thousands were seriously ill, and their ranks would increase sharply by mid-December, thanks to a secondary wave of sickness. Using any conventional standard, the nation's capital had suffered an immense calamity.

And yet, even now, few people in the city had the faintest idea of the extent of the disaster, and many public officials and medical authorities still clung to the comforting illusion that there had actually been no killer smog and that air pollution was not a grave and acute menace to health.

Their attitude was perfectly reflected in a brief leader which appeared in the distinguished British medical publication the *Lancet*. "Our fogs are undoubtedly cleaner than they were, and less of a 'smog' now that electric and gas fires have replaced so many open fires and kitchen ranges. The watch kept on the quality of smokes from factories means that we are unlikely to have such a disaster as happened at Donora, Pennsylvania, in 1948."

The leader appeared in the *Lancet* more than ten days *after* the smog's end.

Thirty-one

ALL DURING the dark hours of Tuesday morning, the mass of cold, polluted air moved slowly on; behind it, the long-delayed low-pressure system pushed forward toward the

Thames valley, and the first fresh winds from south and west stirred through the city, bringing drafts of clean air to mix with the smog.

By dawn the winds had picked up to four and five knots, and the smog, somewhat diluted now, continued to thin. Conditions rapidly improved. Borough after borough began to clear, and by the time that the morning rush hour was well underway, fresh air was flowing into every quarter of the metropolis.

At ten minutes after nine, the Thames was virtually clear of fog for its entire length. As the skies brightened, the men in the Thames Navigation Service at Tilbury and Gravesend witnessed a rare spectacle. Ships of every size and description first raised steam, and then, four abreast, swept past the docks and landings and headed out to sea, past the multitude of ships gathered around the river mouth, waiting to enter. Eighteen large liners and an equal number of smaller ones, 35 coasters and colliers, 20 mudhoppers and tows, and 18 motor barges—109 vessels in all—sailed by in a seemingly endless armada. And when the channel was clear, more than twice as many ships began to enter the Thames—a total of over 240—hastening upstream to the docks and wharves that lined the sides of the river.

Before long, the great Port of London was in full operation again. It had been shut down for one hundred and five hours and ten minutes, the longest recorded period of total inactivity in its history.

As the weather gradually cleared around Greater London, more and more abandoned cars were reclaimed and driven away. Transportation in the city began to return to normal; buses, motor coaches, and the Underground soon were operating without delays, and the railways, both long-distance and suburban, finally returned to a regular schedule.

When London Airport reopened, Jerry Briggs left his office near Fleet Street and took Ethel and Abby to their plane. All in all, he thought, considering the weather and how rotten things had been in the city for most of their visit, Ethel and her friend had worked out pretty well.

The odd thing was that none of them realized at the time what actually had been happening in London. People just didn't know how serious the smog had been. Afterward, when the news finally came out, he and Dot sent Ethel a few clippings, so that at least she'd know that while visiting them in Hampstead, she had lived through something they were beginning to call the "Killer Smog."

≈

The end of the temperature inversion and the dispersal of the polluted air brought no immediate relief to the city's hard-pressed hospitals. On Tuesday, after the smog already had lifted, the Emergency Bed Service was compelled to issue its second-stage "yellow" warning, advising the four regional boards that for more than one out of five patients, a hospital bed no longer could be found. The "yellow" warning remained in effect until the following Monday; not until two days after that, on Wednesday, December 17, did conditions improve sufficiently in the city for the less serious "white" warning to be lifted as well.

The clean air flowing into the city on Tuesday, December 9, proved a godsend to thousands of afflicted Londoners. For other thousands, it arrived too late.

≈

The doctor returned again on Tuesday to the house in Little Stanmore. He agreed with Mary Chapman that her baby had taken a turn for the worse. Arrangements were made to receive him in the nearest hospital, and that night she left Albert in the children's ward, where he would have expert attention.

He did not seem to get any better. On Wednesday, Thursday, Friday, his breathing remained difficult; he ran a low fever; neither the sulfa drugs nor the antibiotics had any effect. The doctor's expression became graver. On Saturday Albert's fever climbed steadily. It reached 104.

She and John remained in the hospital all that day, and late in the afternoon, someone came and told them their baby was dead.

Afterward, they went back to their own house in Hammersmith. That night, after stirring the fire, John looked out the window and said, "The fog killed him. If it hadn't gotten so bad, you know, and lasted so long, Albert would still be alive."

It was true, of course. And yet, Mary Chapman thought, saying it didn't make things any better. The house was so empty now. And so very damp. Only it didn't really matter any more if it was damp or not.

In South Norwood, Mrs. Wilcox began to improve almost as soon as the fog had lifted. She remained quite pale and thin, however, and Dr. Speyer told her niece that he thought the patient's recovery might take considerable time.

By the fifteenth of the month, she had developed pneumonia. She was in hospital when Mr. Wilcox came home from his ship. So they were together for Christmas, though hardly the way she had originally planned it.

Early in January she was able to leave the hospital, but it wasn't for long. Her lungs had been severely affected by the smog and were susceptible to infection. She suffered a relapse in late January and returned to the hospital with a second case of pneumonia. Dr. Speyer watched her closely, knowing that she was hanging on by a thread.

Mrs. Wilcox slowly grew better, as some smog victims did. Her health remained shaky, though, all through the spring and summer; she did not recover completely until a year after she had been stricken.

By Christmas, 1953, Dr. Speyer could tell his patient that she was finally out of danger. The only limits on her future activities would be during a period of fog. At that time she should at all costs stay indoors and shut the house up as tightly as she could.

He told her something else that he had not mentioned

before. "You were lucky last year," he said. "That first night—if your niece hadn't been staying in the house with you, if you'd been living alone—you would have been one of those they found dead in the morning."

Mrs. Wilcox never doubted that he was right. Or stopped counting herself fortunate that her niece had had a four-week-old baby and an ice-cold flat with a hopelessly blocked up flue.

Once the smog had finally disappeared from the city, many a healthy Londoner forgot almost everything about it, except, perhaps, for a single, sharp physical impression. A lady in Chelsea might recall that on the night when the smog had been at its worst, the street lamp outside her bedroom window had disappeared completely; a gentleman in Kensington might remember that one afternoon he had gone out for some tobacco and had very nearly been sick to his stomach afterward.

There was one member of the Metropolitan Police who had a different sort of recollection. It concerned something he saw on Wednesday, the day after the smog lifted.

The previous afternoon, a man's body had been found floating in the Thames; it had been there for at least ten or twelve days, according to the medical examiner.

On Wednesday the police officer went to Southwark, to be present while relatives identified the deceased. The officer had steadied himself in advance for the unpleasant task, but not for the sight that greeted him inside the mortuary.

The low, windowless room was crowded with corpses. Casualties, he realized at once, of the dense fog which had blanketed the city all during the past weekend.

It wasn't their numbers, though, that startled him. It was the way they were lying there, on various benches and tables, their exposed faces turned upward to the ceiling, and none of them, as far as he could see, wrapped up for burial yet.

An attendant explained the situation. The matter was really quite simple. There was nothing left to wrap the corpses *in*. So many people had died during the fog that the Borough of Southwark had used up its supply of shrouds.

Part Three–
Aftermath of the Smog

". . . in the London episode the air pollutants, when considered in terms of their human effects, closely resembled those present in the air of many other urban areas. . . . For example, although Los Angeles air pollution is chemically different from that of London the two resemble each other in their effects on man since each causes irritation of exposed living membranes."

Chapter titled: "Effects on Human Health,"
H. Heimann, in AIR POLLUTION,
World Health Organization,
Geneva, 1961.

Chapter Thirty-two

IMMEDIATELY AFTER the killer smog had lifted, London found itself a prey to rumor and confusion. At first, only one thing was certain—the city had experienced an extraordinarily dense, obnoxious, and prolonged pea-souper, but how damaging it might have been to the health of the inhabitants, no one could say. As yet not a single government official realized that tens of thousands had been made seriously ill or that the final death toll would be placed, perhaps somewhat conservatively, at four thousand victims.

Little by little, however, an outline of the tragedy began to emerge. The popular newspapers sensed that there was a "story" in the recent smog—in all likelihood a sensational one—and they went after it diligently. If their accounts were often inaccurate, they at least served the purpose of alerting the public for the first time to the extreme menace of polluted air.

On December 12, three days after the smog's end, the

Daily Express revealed that London's hospitals were crowded with patients suffering from what the newspaper called a a "mysterious fog illness." Doctors were said to be uncertain whether the "epidemic" had been caused by an infection or by the irritating nature of the fog.

Two days later, the *Sunday Dispatch* reported a new and disturbing rumor—that a thousand people had died as a result of the smog. In addition, ambulances were still answering a hundred extra calls a day, mainly from asthma sufferers; emergency beds were in use in many hospitals; and "one of the worst funeral hold-ups since the 1918 flu epidemic" was causing distress to both relatives of the dead and to the city's heavily overworked morticians.

And then, in the House of Commons, Mr. Ian Macleod, the nation's Minister of Health, made a shocking revelation. During the week ending December 13, approximately three thousand excess deaths had been recorded in Greater London; because there was no evidence of influenza or other epidemic disease, these excess deaths could only be blamed on the great killer smog.

From this point on, it was impossible to deny that the smog had been a cruel and devastating calamity and that for at least four days and nights the citizens of one of the world's proudest cities had been exposed to a modern version of the plague. Surely, now, it was reasonable to suppose that the government would undertake an immediate investigation of the tragedy itself and that this would be promptly followed by corrective legislation to control air pollution.

The conduct of the government was of concern not only to Londoners themselves but to city dwellers around the globe. For by 1952 smog already was a serious problem in almost every advanced nation in the world, and what now happened in Parliament and Whitehall very likely would provide a blueprint for the general future. The real issue at stake was this: in the face of immense and mounting difficulties, could modern government find the means, the desire, and the will to begin safeguarding the health and lives of its urban population—or had polluted air, sickness, and death become the inescapable price that had to be paid for the benefits of a highly industrialized society?

The events which now took place in the capital could not have been reassuring to even the most optimistic observer.

Thirty-three

BY MID-DECEMBER, 1952, although it was clear that London had suffered an acute air pollution disaster, incredibly enough the government's first decision was to do nothing whatever about it. On December 17 and 18, two Members of the House of Commons, Mr. Norman Dodds and Mr. Tom Driberg, urged an immediate inquiry; their proposals were rejected. Further questions and demands for action were subsequently put to the government's Ministers, but always with the same essential response: everything was being done that was required, no special investigation was desirable, and while the subject of air pollution was certainly an important one, all necessary steps to deal with the problem already were being taken by existing committees, scientific bodies, and by the government itself.

The critics would not be silenced, though, and before long they had additional ammunition. In early January, 1953, an article appeared in the highly respected *British Medical Journal*, suggesting that as many as 4,700 deaths had been caused by the smog. Later in the same month, the London County Council issued its annual medical report; included was the impressive and quite valid assertion that the killer smog had probably been more deadly than the worst nineteenth-century outbreak of cholera.

Armed with these new disclosures, Mr. Dodds, at the end of January, resumed his role of gadfly in the Commons, questioning the Minister of Housing and Local Government,

Mr. Harold Macmillan, about the lack of official action. "Does the Minister appreciate," Mr. Dodds asked, "that last month, in Greater London alone, there were literally more people choked to death by air pollution than were killed on the roads of the whole country in 1952? Why is a public inquiry not being held?"

No persuasive answer was received. Mr. Barnett Janner then asked the same Minister if he would consider introducing general legislation to deal with the air pollution problem? Mr. Macmillan replied that he "was not satisfied that further general legislation [was] needed at present," and pointed out that the drafting of any new laws would be extremely challenging, because "an enormous number of broad economic considerations" would be involved.

The implication of the Minister's remarks, a number of people felt, was that the government viewed the air pollution problem as so difficult to deal with that it hoped, through delaying tactics, not to have to deal with it at all. The exchange was concluded by Mr. Dodds, who declared that he found the government guilty of "an amazing display of apathy," and promised to raise the subject again at the first opportunity.

In early February, under questioning in the Commons, a last, eye-catching statistic was elicited from a reluctant Minister of Pensions and National Insurance. In Greater London, during December, 1952, twenty-five thousand more claims for sickness benefits had been received than during the corresponding month of the previous year; no less than ten thousand of these could be ascribed only to the smog.

But the number of those made seriously ill had obviously been far larger than ten thousand; sickness benefits were applied for by the working population alone; excluded were housewives, children, the elderly, and those unable to work because of prior disabilities—the most vulnerable members of the community. While one estimate, made in Parliament, was undoubtedly inflated—that a million Londoners had suffered serious illness because of the smog—it would hardly seem an exaggeration to suppose that between

50,000 and 100,000 people had been made sick to some degree after breathing the city's polluted air for four consecutive days and nights.

Still, the government refused to take action, and the main reason for its inertia was not hard to find. As one well-informed Member of Parliament was to remark afterward, when the struggle began in early 1953, "there were no votes to be gained from scouring the atmosphere." Until there was evidence of widespread public demand for clean air, there would be no special committee appointed, no subsequent recommendations, and no effective legislation enacted in Parliament.

The reformers had never been in a more favorable position, though. Almost overnight, the grisly events of December had vindicated their cause and gained for their principal organization, the National Smoke Abatement Society, the approval and respect it too long had been denied. Nor did the Society intend to let its best opportunity slip by. Abundant information was supplied to the newspapers, so that the killer smog and the whole air pollution problem would not be forgotten. Society members made speeches, and wrote major articles for the press; both activities had their impact.

Even more effective in awakening public opinion was a survey of the smog disaster which appeared in the spring issue of the Society's journal, *Smokeless Air*. Copies were sent to government officials and to all Members of Parliament. The survey contained a summary of the weather factors during the smog, the amount of pollution in the air, an analysis of deaths and illness, and, perhaps most important of all, an estimate of the economic cost of the disaster. The city of London, according to the Society, would have to pay roughly ten million pounds, or almost thirty million dollars, in depreciation, expenses, and lost time as a result of the four-day smog.

The survey stirred such broad interest that copies were soon exhausted, and a special reprinting had to be ordered to meet the demand.

Pressure for government action continued to mount during the spring, and on May 8, Mr. Dodds led another assault in the Commons. The most significant part of his speech concerned the mail he had been receiving from his constituents.

"Since I became a Member of Parliament in 1945," Mr. Dodds declared, "I have certainly had a great deal of correspondence, but I have never had more correspondence on any subject than I have on this question of air pollution. One letter states: 'May I offer my praise for your stand for the end of this disgraceful complacency and indifference to the shocking pollution of our air? The deaths caused by the recent fog, though awful, were nothing compared with the thousands whose lungs were damaged to a lesser extent, perhaps to prove fatal at a later date.'"

The public was aroused and fearful; this was the key to what happened next. The government's reply to Mr. Dodds was that it had "decided to appoint a committee under an independent chairman, to undertake a comprehensive review of the causes and effects of air pollution, and to consider what further preventive measures are practicable."

The first battle had been won by the reformers, but their victory had been gained over a grudging foe, and they had little reason to believe that the remainder of the struggle would be swift, easy, or necessarily successful. Soon a fresh delay reinforced their doubts; ten more weeks elapsed before a government spokesman was able to announce, with ostensible enthusiasm, that a "strong" Air Pollution Committee had been formed and that its chairman would be the extremely capable and widely respected Sir Hugh Beaver.

If mistrust of the government's motives remained strong, the Ministers had only themselves to blame. More than seven months had passed since the end of the great killer smog, and only now was an interdepartmental committee about to begin its investigations.

Thirty-four

IT WAS EXTREMELY fortunate for the reformers that a man of Sir Hugh Beaver's knowledge and attainments had agreed to serve as the impartial chairman of the government's Air Pollution Committee. Sir Hugh was a practical man who had traveled widely as a consulting engineer; in 1931, at the request of the Prime Minister of Canada, he had taken responsibility for rebuilding the harbor of Saint John, New Brunswick, after its destruction by fire. Knighted in 1943, he became, three years later, the managing director of Arthur Guinness Son and Company, the internationally famous brewing firm. Since the war, he had served on several parliamentary commissions and during 1951-52 had been chairman of the Committee on Power Station Construction, a useful apprenticeship for his present task.

In addition, he had visited the United States some thirty times and had been in Donora, Pennsylvania, in 1947, the year before that city's smog disaster. It was no serious drawback that in July, 1953, when he assumed the chairmanship of what was to become known as the Beaver Committee, he had only a limited understanding of the technical problems of air pollution control; these details he quickly mastered. Far more important, he brought to the committee a vast amount of administrative experience in governmental, financial, and scientific affairs—an experience that was essential if the committee's work was to be conducted successfully and its recommendations were to lead to meaningful legislation.

It did not take Sir Hugh very long to make an accurate appraisal of the situation confronting him. Experts in a variety of fields would have to be consulted, dozens of hearings and discussions would have to be held, and only then—

after perhaps a year, or even two—would the committee be in a position to present its complete findings. Sir Hugh believed that the government hoped the public's furor would subside in the meantime, and that the demand for air pollution reform would be forgotten.

The chairman had no intention of letting this happen or of allowing the Beaver Committee to become an innocent party to the scheme. He devised a counterstrategy—as a holding operation the committee would publish an *Interim Report,* written in simple, nontechnical language, that the country's newspapers could quote extensively and that the man-in-the-street could readily understand. The chairman's aim was to reach the widest possible audience and to keep public opinion fully aroused until a *Final Report* could be published with legislative recommendations.

By late autumn, Sir Hugh decided it was time to act; almost a year had passed since the December disaster, and the public's interest was beginning to flag. He invited the ten members of his committee to join him one Saturday morning at London's most famous club, the Atheneum. There, in a private room overlooking Waterloo Place, and within sight of the statue of a melancholy Florence Nightingale holding her lamp, the chairman informed his associates that the moment had come to put their preliminary findings on record; the members might depart whenever they wished, but he himself intended to remain until the work was done. By Sunday night only the chairman and two others were still present, but the report was written and ready for the press.

In December, 1953, the Beaver Committee's *Interim Report* was officially released. Afterward, it was widely quoted and discussed, and during the next ten or twelve months its effect on the public was very much what the chairman had desired. The report consisted of two parts, a technical survey of the air pollution problem and recommendations for immediate action to be taken to prevent another smog disaster. These included warning bulletins from the Meteorological Office whenever smog conditions were likely to prevail; gauze masks for the elderly and for those suffering from heart or chest disease; a campaign to persuade people to remain indoors as much as possible, with their houses tightly sealed; a ban on the burning of rubbish and the lighting of bonfires; the urging of the public not to drive their cars into thickly settled urban areas; and the use of smokeless fuel during heavy fog periods.

By implication, the Beaver Committee's *Interim Report* found both national and local government guilty of negligence in failing to take all possible steps to protect the people of London from a smog disaster. At the same time, the report also made it quite clear that the average Londoner had to accept a part of the responsibility for smog conditions and that he was unjustified in blaming neighboring factories and generating stations for all the dirty air in the city. "The appropriate authorities," the report said, "should . . . bring to the notice of the public . . . that the largest single producer of smoke is the domestic consumer." It was this fact, clearly announced, and for the first time widely circulated, that convinced many Britons of the menace in their own open coal fires and of the necessity to eliminate them as quickly as possible.

The government appeared to welcome the *Interim Report* and promised to implement its recommendations. But the chairman remained skeptical of Whitehall's real intentions. He could not easily forget that the Minister of Housing and Local Government, who represented the department most concerned with the air pollution problem, had failed to consult with him on even a single occasion during the first eight months of his committee's existence. Sir Hugh was familiar enough with administrative procedures to understand the implications. The government was still indifferent to reform, still hoped that the subject would be forgotten.

It was another year before the Beaver Committee's *Final Report* made its appearance. During that time, the chairman remained under harassment from two directions.

On one side, there was sniping from the enemies of air pollution control—the coal merchants, the manufacturers of open fire grates, the electricity producers, and those individual boiler operators, many of them elderly, who feared that they would be unable to meet the higher work-standards proposed, even after retraining. On the opposite side, the committee was attacked by the fanatical wing of the reformers, those recent converts to the cause of clean air who insisted that the nation's atmosphere be purified overnight and who were interested only in an "all-or-nothing" approach. It was not enough for these zealots that the Beaver Committee proposed to drastically reduce smoke; a parallel reduction of sulfur dioxide had to be made simultaneously. Until the technical means could be found to accomplish this impossible task, the extremists wanted no reforms at all.

The chairman steered a middle course between the two, and in November, 1954, when the *Final Report* was published, it offered the government and the nation a well-organized and practical plan for the immediate future. Recommendations included the elimination of black smoke from all chimneys, including those in private dwellings, the control of industrial emissions, the production of greater supplies of smokeless fuels and a scheme for their distribution, the reduction of railway nuisances, and the establishment of smokeless zones in urban areas—the last, an innovation first proposed in 1935 by the Smoke Abatement Society. The report further recommended "that clean air should be declared a national policy . . . recognized by the Government," and looked forward to a time, ten or fifteen years in the future, when sulfur dioxide could begin to be effectively curbed and when smoke in Britain's Black Areas and cities, including London, would have been reduced by 70 or 80 percent.

The plan proposed in the *Final Report* was the most vigorous and comprehensive ever drawn up by a parliamentary committee, and the public's insistence on clean air had never been so strong. But even now, there was no guarantee that the Beaver Committee had actually accomplished anything. The government was not yet committed publicly to a Clean Air Act, and there remained a strong belief that no official action would be forthcoming.

In November, 1954, two years after the great killer smog, these doubts were expressed in an informative British journal called the *Municipal Review*. The article said, ". . . in a government office there is a nice, clean, empty pigeon-hole the same size and shape as the Beaver Report, and there are probably several nice, clean and tidy politicians who . . . would like to see this report suitably housed."

Somehow the government had to be forced to act. A last battle had to be waged—and now it was—in the nation's Parliament.

Thirty-five

WITH THE PUBLICATION of the Beaver Committee's *Final Report*, six Tory and six Labor Members of the Commons met informally and established a nonpartisan alliance. Their aim was to compel the government to introduce an effective Clean Air Measure, based on the Beaver Committee's findings. But to accomplish this, the twelve M.P.'s realized they would need more than an ordinary amount of good luck.

Periodically, a lottery is held in the House of Commons; those drawing winning numbers are then privileged to introduce a "Private Member's Bill," if they choose to do so. The twelve M.P.'s agreed that if one of their number should become a lottery winner, he would introduce a Clean Air Bill as a private measure, with the eleven others acting as his "backers." Such a move, it was felt, would place tremendous pressure on the government; it would act as a "pistol at the Ministers' backs," as the *Manchester Guardian* described it, and ultimately would force the government either to take over the private bill itself or to offer a comprehensive measure of its own.

The next lottery was held a few days afterward. The slips of paper were placed inside the large, black box used on such occasions, they were shuffled about, and then the Clerk of the Table drew out the first winning number. At that moment, fate smiled upon the reformers. The Speaker announced the name of the first winner; it was Mr. Gerald Nabarro, Tory Member for Kidderminster—one of the leaders of the alliance.

Mr. Nabarro was probably the ideal Member to present a Clean Air Bill. He was energetic, determined, thorough; he was also one of the best speakers in the House, a man of such forensic talents that the *Daily Mail* once described him as "one of a star-spangled trio who could pack the Commons with Tory and Labour M.P.'s within seconds after their names appeared on the board—the other two: Winston Churchill and Aneurin Bevan."

The Member for Kidderminster lost little time in seeking assistance. Early in December, he approached the National Smoke Abatement Society. He informed the Society's officers that he proposed to introduce a Clean Air Measure as a Private Member's Bill, based on the legislative recommendations of the Beaver Committee. He needed briefing from the Society on the entire air pollution question; he needed expert help in drafting his proposed bill, and most vital of all, he needed money to pay for his expenses. A few days later, the Society's executive council agreed to provide the assistance required and to help Mr. Nabarro in his preparations.

On one question, though, there was substantial disagreement between the Member for Kidderminster and the Society. The latter favored a proposal that would be limited in scope; Mr. Nabarro insisted that his bill be made as broad as possible, so that the government could not escape the choice of taking the measure over or of introducing an equally broad measure of its own.

No decision on this point had been reached in late

January when the government reacted officially, for the first time, to the Beaver *Report*. On the twenty-fifth, the recently appointed Minister of Housing and Local Government, Mr. Duncan Sandys, indicated that Whitehall looked with favor on the *Report* and was prepared to accept, in principle, the policy it recommended. Discussions already were taking place, Mr. Sandys added, with both local authorities and representatives of industry. But no positive government commitment was made, no mention was heard of legislative proposals, and the suspicion lingered that government was still planning to act cautiously—if at all.

Within forty-eight hours, Mr. Nabarro moved again; meeting with the Smoke Abatement Society's executive council, he explained in detail the contents and purpose of his bill and won the members' unqualified endorsement.

Eight days later, a packed House of Commons prepared to hear the Second Reading of Mr. Nabarro's Clean Air Bill. Excitement ran high—thanks, in considerable part, to the publicity the bill's sponsor had deliberately sought during the preceding weeks. Mr. Nabarro was a modern reformer who believed in modern methods; he had called a press conference to explain his bill, and then had taken the unusual step of having his own parliamentary letters stamped with the legend: "Gerald Nabarro's Clean Air (Anti-smog) Bill, Second Reading, Friday, February 4, 1955." At 11:15 A.M., the Member for Kidderminster rose and addressed the House. He spoke for 43 eloquent minutes, and then was followed by a number of other Members, almost all speaking in favor of the bill.

But even now, opinion was not unanimous. The great killer smog had failed to convince Mr. Michael Higgs, Member for Bromsgrove, of the need for air pollution reform. Mr. Higgs objected to the supposed invasion of personal privacy which he felt was implied in the bill; he also confessed to a bias. "I am," he said, "one who has a great liking for a pleasant, open coal fire on a Sunday afternoon or evening. . . ." There was, happily, little support for Mr. Higgs's point of view.

A few minutes afterward, Whitehall's position was at last made clear by the Minister of Housing and Local Government. Addressing himself to the House, Mr. Sandys said that he did not advise the Members to accept the measure. He stressed that it had been prepared without consulting the various interested parties, that it contained drafting defects, and that because it was a Private Member's Bill, it could not provide the necessary financial provisions. He also suggested that there might be a question of constitutionality, if the bill were to be taken over by the government at a subsequent stage of its consideration.

All of which was actually a prelude to capitulation; for the Minister then promised that after further consultations, and within a reasonable period of time, the government would present a bill of its own, based on the Beaver Committee's recommendations.

With the government finally committed to a Clean Air Act, Mr. Nabarro withdrew his Private Member's Bill—in triumph.

Before the pledge could be carried out, Sir Winston Churchill retired as Prime Minister, and a new general election was held, with both Labor and Tory parties including air pollution reform in their election platforms. A Tory victory was followed by the fulfillment of this promise, and the Clean Air Act became law, on July 5, 1956.

It might truly be said that the beginning of an effective air pollution control program had been a long time coming. By now, 137 years had passed since the first modern parliamentary committee had made a study of the problem, almost four hundred since Elizabeth I had complained of the brewery smoke invading her palace at Westminster, and more than seven hundred since the early London coal merchants had established themselves in business along rural Sacoles Lane. By 1956, the patient British people certainly deserved to have something done about purifying the air they breathed.

Yet a Clean Air Bill had almost not been written and enacted into law. Without good luck in a lottery drawing and without Gerald Nabarro's Private Member's Bill, there might have been no reform. A number of contemporary commentators, among them Sir Hugh Beaver himself, certainly believed so; had it not been for the Nabarro Bill, they said, the government probably would have avoided action for many months and might have avoided it entirely.

Whether true or not, hardly anyone could deny that reform was long overdue. To underline the point, early in 1956, the same year in which the Clean Air Act was passed, a new killer smog invaded the capital. This time the effects were somewhat less disastrous. Perhaps because of more favorable meteorological conditions, "only" one thousand people died. As always, there was no way of telling how many others were made seriously ill.

Thirty-six

THE GREAT KILLER SMOG descended on London more than fifteen years ago. Since then, the problems which it so vividly and tragically exemplified have grown far worse, and the world's limited supply of air has become increasingly contaminated. Current trends are unfavorable—so much so, that it is almost impossible to exaggerate the gravity of the air pollution crisis. One of America's leading meteorologists has described the situation by saying, "If present concentrations continue to be poured into the air without controls, no human on earth will be able to exist."

Reducing air pollution is no simple or easy task. Ten years of reform under the Clean Air Act, with the implementation of a new national fuel policy and the development of an expensive, government-sponsored control program, has left London and Great Britain's other large cities with air that is anything but clean.

Many Britons will tell you that conditions are better

than they were—which is true—but how much actual improvement there has been, remains open to question. Britain's cities, in common with others of Europe and America, continue to grow in size and population, while fuel consumption continues to increase. Though coal smoke has been reduced by 50 percent throughout Britain, sulfur dioxide emissions are far greater than they were ten years ago. And previously unforeseen problems have grown up at an alarming rate; in 1960, nine million motor vehicles were licensed in Great Britain; by 1965, there were thirteen million, and in crowded urban areas, particularly the capital, there were "tremendous increases in the pollution of air near ground level." The economic cost of contaminated air in Britain remains staggeringly high—at more than a billion dollars a year. The cost in human health cannot be measured.

In America the situation may be even more critical. The atmosphere over much of the eastern half of the country is chronically polluted. Every large American city suffers from dirty air. Residents of New York, Chicago, Los Angeles, St. Louis, and Philadelphia are said to endure the worst conditions, but they are certainly not the only millions affected. In all, according to current government estimates, there are more than sixty large urban areas in the United States with extremely serious air pollution problems, and probably no American city of more than fifty thousand inhabitants enjoys clean air the year round.

To date, the nation's efforts to meet its air pollution problems have been almost totally inadequate. Recently a new measure was passed by Congress and signed into law. *The Wall Street Journal* said of it, approvingly, "The air pollution control bill the Senate passed the other day represents a victory for business spokesmen." Unfortunately, it did. But not a victory for the average American city dweller, who apparently cannot yet depend on his own national government to deal decisively with the burgeoning problems of contaminated air. To complete the dismal picture, there are far too few regional and local laws that even exist, and those that do are generally quite ineffective.

Perhaps, as in Great Britain, change will begin to come only after a large-scale tragedy. The conditions are favorable for one in any of a dozen of the nation's most populous cities. A mass of still air drifting slowly eastward, an intense thermal inversion, and then five, six, seven days of increasingly poisonous smog. The air will look bronze, almost copper-colored, as it did during New York's 1966 Thanksgiving smog. It will smell "smoky" to some, while to others it will seem to be "distinctly sulfurous." Thousands will notice a burning sensation in their eyes; other thousands will develop symptoms of bronchitis or asthma for the first time; additional hundreds—or even thousands—will suffer heart failure or choke to death for lack of oxygen. And when the mortality statistics have been collected and analyzed, the rest of the country will read in its newspapers and hear on its television sets about a vast new killer smog—and demand an end to government's indifference and delay.

The citizens of London did not believe themselves to be in danger, on the fifth of December, 1952. In a hundred calamitous hours, the great killer smog proved that they were wrong. From every appearance, a similar tragedy is now being prepared in America—and there is very little time left in which to prevent it.

BIBLIOGRAPHY

Air Pollution. World Health Organization, Geneva: 1961.

Britain: An Official Handbook. The Central Office of Information, 1966.

Defoe, Daniel. *Tour Through the Whole Island of Great Britain.* London: G. Strahan, 1724-27.

Doyle, A. Conan. *His Last Bow.* London: John Murray, Ltd., 1917.

Eades, Geo. E. *Historic London: The Story of a City and Its People.* London: Queen Anne Press Ltd. and City of London Society, 1966.

Evelyn, John. *Fumifugium.* 1661. Reissued under the title: *The Smoke of London.* Oxford: R. T. Gunther, 1930.

George, M. D. *London Life in the XVIIIth Century.* New York: Alfred A. Knopf, Inc., 1925.

Golden Milestone: 50 Years of the AA. The Automobile Association, 1955.

Low, D. M. *London is London;* A Selection of Prose and Verse. London: Chatto & Windus, 1949.

Marsh, Arnold. *Smoke; The Problem of Coal and the Atmosphere.* London: Faber & Faber, Ltd., 1947.

Marshal, W. A. L. *A Century of London Weather.* London: H. M. Stationery Office, 1952.

Mitchell, R. J. and Leys, M. D. R. *History of London Life.* London: Longmans, Green & Co., Ltd., 1958.

Political Studies, Vol IX, No. 3. Oxford: Clarendon Press, October, 1961.

Roueche, Berton. *Eleven Blue Men, and Other Narratives of Medical Detection.* New York: Berkley Medallion Books, 1953.

Thomson, David. *England in the Nineteenth Century, 1815-1914.* London: Cape (Jonathan), Ltd., 1964.

Thomson, David. *England in the Twentieth Century, 1914-1963.* London: Cape (Jonathan), Ltd., 1964.

Trevelyan, George Macauley. *History of England.* London: Longmans, Green & Co., Ltd., 1926.

Reports

Report. Departmental Committee on Smoke and Noxious Vapours Abatement (The Newton Committee). Ministry of Health, 1921.

Domestic Fuel Policy. Fuel and Power Advisory Council (The Simon Committee), 1946.

Interim Report. Committee on Air Pollution (The Beaver Committee). H. M. Stationery Office. December, 1953.

The 1952 Fog in a Metropolitan Borough. E. H. R. Smithard. Medical Officer of Health, Lewisham, 1953.

Report of the County Medical Officer of Health. London County Council, 1953.

Report. Committee on Air Pollution (The Beaver Committee). H. M. Stationery Office. November, 1954.

No. 95. *Mortality and Morbidity During the London Fog of December, 1952.* Ministry of Health. Reports on Public Health and Medical Subjects. H. M. Stationery Office, 1954.

Parliamentary Debates. 5th Series. (Hansard) Commons: H. M. Stationery Office.

Presidential Addresses. Annual Meetings, National Society for Smoke Abatement.

Newspapers, Periodicals, Etc.:

British Broadcasting Corporation, Transcripts of Broadcasts.

British Medical Journal.

Daily Express.

Daily Mail.

Daily Mirror.

Edinburgh Evening News.

Evening News, The.

Journal of the Royal Sanitary Institute.

Lancet.

Manchester Guardian.

Medical Officer.

Municipal Review.

New York Herald Tribune.

New York Times, The.

Smokeless Air—Quarterly Journal of the National Smoke Abatement Society.

Sunday Dispatch.

Sunday Times, The.

Times, The.

Wall Street Journal, The.

About the Author—

William Wise was born in New York City and was graduated from Yale University. He is well-known writer of books for children and young adults. His adult fiction has appeared in *Town & Country*, *Harper's* and the *Yale Review*. He has also reviewed books for the *Saturday Review* and *The New York Times*.

9 780595 171842

Made in the USA
Monee, IL
24 August 2022

12410295R00111